RISJ *CHALLENGES*

Are Foreign Correspondents Redundant?

The changing face of international news

Richard Sambrook

REUTERS
INSTITUTE for the
STUDY of
JOURNALISM

UNIVERSITY OF
OXFORD

Contents

Executive Summary 1

1. The Changing Role of the Foreign Correspondent 3

2. Economics 11

3. Technology 27

4. Globalisation 47

5. The Public Appetite for Foreign News 59

6. On the Ground: Introducing the Case Studies 69

7. China: The Dragon Stirs 71

8. Africa: Learning to Report Itself 81

9. Iran: The Closed Society 89

10. Case Study Conclusions 95

11. Conclusions 97

List of Interviewees 103

Bibliography 105

Acknowledgements 107

Executive Summary

Foreign news is undergoing a transformation. For more than a hundred years the principal means of learning about events in the rest of the world has been through the reporting of journalists based abroad. The model of a foreign correspondent, working from a fixed overseas bureau, is well established across all forms of international newsgathering – newspapers, wire agencies, broadcasters. It is a feature which grew from the industrialisation of news production in the late nineteenth century, when a limited number of organisations had sufficient resources to gather and distribute news, with owners seeking the prestige and influence that reporting international events brings.

However, there was news from abroad before there were correspondents and bureaux. And we are now entering a new era where they may no longer be central to how we learn about the world. A wide range of pressures are undermining the role of foreign correspondent and providing opportunities – and imperatives – for news organisations to adopt a very different approach to reporting international news.

As John Maxwell Hamilton notes in his book *Journalism's Roving Eye,* 'The latest phase in the evolution of foreign news has come with a wrenching swiftness not seen since the beginnings of the mass media penny press.' The economic pressures of maintaining overseas newsgathering have seen the numbers of bureaux and correspondents persistently reduced by major Western news organisations over the last 20 years or more. This has led to a downward spiral in the quantity of international news being reported – particularly in the USA.

It is principally a Western phenomenon. In Asia, with the prospect of major economic growth, news organisations may be set for an era of expansion. And in the developing world countries and continents are building their own journalistic capacity – with long-term consequences for the global flow of information and the character of public debate.

At the same time digital technology has transformed both the gathering and distribution of news, providing, among other things, the opportunity

1

for a 'networked' and more open model for reporting international affairs, with internet blogs, aggregators, and new models of low-cost online news and information.

Social media are leading, supplementing and complementing what professional news organisations offer, providing fresh source material for reporters, but also competing with them for public attention. Many other organisations have taken the opportunity to contribute directly to public debate by introducing their own information services – from governments, to NGOs to commercial companies – speaking directly to the public in favour of their own interests. This challenges the capacities of news organisations to sort, verify and contextualise a torrent of digital information.

Finally, globalisation has also led to significant changes in how the world is reported. In multicultural societies the notion of 'foreign' is more complex. International and domestic news agendas have merged to a significant degree. More organisations are relying on local staff – with advantages and risks attached.

As this combination of forces changes the way we learn and think about the world, the challenges for news organisations include:

- Adopting new roles as the value in foreign reporting shifts to the extremes of breaking news and in-depth specialism.

- Rethinking the international agenda as news values change and 'bottom–up' priorities emerge; using digital technology to broaden coverage.

- Entering new partnerships with a more open and networked approach as vertically integrated news operations break down.

- Innovating in the digital sphere or risk being outflanked by new entrants.

- Finding new economic models which can sustain international operations.

- Training and recruiting to provide the expertise and cultural flexibility needed in the twenty-first-century news arena.

All news organisations are undergoing turbulent change and must ask where the risks and the opportunities are. And against this background, where does the primary public interest rest in 'bearing witness'?

Are foreign correspondents redundant?

1. The Changing Role of the Foreign Correspondent

William Howard Russell's reports for *The Times* from the Crimean War in 1854 are frequently cited as one of the first examples of a professional foreign correspondent. Whether, as his epitaph in St Paul's Cathedral declares, he was the 'first and the greatest' war correspondent is open to debate.[1] However, he does represent one of the earliest and best known examples of a correspondent being deployed abroad to report on international events of national interest.

His Managing Editor, Mowbray Morris, wrote:

> *The public expects that we shall have our own agents ... And it has long been accustomed to look to The Times ... for the truth in all things. We disappoint a reasonable expectation when we offer nothing better than reports from other journals, however authentic.*[2]

It is a public expectation which holds true today in the age of 24-hour satellite news and the internet. Reporting of international events is expected to be provided by independent journalists employed for that purpose by a news organisation.

However, news from afar was a tradition stretching back to the earliest days of print. The regular production of newspapers or pamphlets was established by the early eighteenth century. And from those earliest days news from abroad was a feature, as Anthony Smith explains in his history:

> *One important aspect of early news publication is that it began not within a small local compass but as an instrument*

---

[1] P. Knightley, *The First Casualty* (2003), 3.
[2] *The History of The Times* (1935–52), ii. 168, cited by Knightley, *First Casualty*, ii. 169.

for describing events across immense geographical areas. In
the societies of Europe it planted in the mind of the individual
literate citizen the picture of a world of public events which
he could never see or experience for himself. It placed his own
society within the context of the continent and the world.[3]

These reports took advantage of well-established, if rudimentary, systems of distribution.

Since the late Middle Ages a formal network of
correspondents and intelligence agents had come into being
across the bulk of the European continent, busily sending
news of military, diplomatic and ecclesiastical affairs along a
series of prescribed routes.[4]

In the nineteenth century overseas news was customarily taken from foreign journals or from 'letters from abroad' sent back by any interested party. See, for example, the letters from writer Anthony Trollope published by the *Liverpool Mercury* in 1875, recounting his extensive travels in the USA, Africa and Australia. Trollope explains that he hopes

by diligence I might be able to do something towards creating
a clearer knowledge of these colonies, I have visited them
all. Of each of them I have given some short account and
have endeavoured to describe the advancing or decreasing
prosperity of their various interests. I hope I have done this
without prejudice.[5]

Much, then as now, was driven by commerce. The same *Liverpool Mercury*, an English regional newspaper with little circulation outside Britain, dispatched the owner's son to the USA to ensure cotton prices were accurately reported back across the Atlantic.

The arrival of the telegraph distributed information around the country from ships arriving at the major ports and developed a commercial advantage in being the first to obtain the latest information. This in time led to the creation of news agencies like Reuters and the Associated Press (AP) who syndicated news to offer international coverage while keeping down the costs to individual subscribers (although it still took almost two weeks for news of Lincoln's assassination to reach Europe by boat in 1865 – a year before the first

---

[3] Smith, *The Newspaper: An International History* (1979), 13.
[4] Ibid. 18.
[5] *The Tireless Traveller* (University of California Press, 1941), 5.

transatlantic cable). The news agencies remain one of the principal sources of international news around the world today.

Prestige and influence drove much of the investment in international reporting. In 1896 William Randolph Hearst sent a reporter to Cuba to report the tensions with the USA as part of an escalating circulation war and, when the reporter cabled there would be no war and he wished to return, Hearst famously responded: 'Please remain. You furnish the pictures, I'll furnish the war'[6] (a message which never reached the correspondent who returned to New York).

The ideological battles of the early twentieth century, with the rise of communism and fascism, and two world wars, cemented the necessity for international reporting for most Western news organisations and led to the establishment of international bureaux and staff correspondents to guarantee the provision of reliable news.

According to John Maxwell Hamilton:

> *The years between the two world wars were a golden age for foreign correspondence. News was momentous. News outlets were plentiful. Living costs abroad were low … In no era have so many correspondents travelled so widely and so freely, many as highly independent freelancers.*[7]

Typical of these was Martha Gellhorn who launched her career in Paris in 1930: 'Having checked the telephone directory, I presented myself at the office of the *New York Times*, and informed the bureau chief … that I was prepared to start work as a foreign correspondent on his staff.'[8] Her reporting of the Spanish Civil War, alongside Ernest Hemingway and photographer Robert Capa, contributed to the aura of romance that still surrounds the idea of the foreign correspondent.

But it was the Second World War that reinforced the weight and significance of the role, perhaps best epitomised by the CBS correspondent Ed Murrow, reporting from London. According to his biographer A. M. Sperber,

> *The voice of Edward R Murrow was a living link between North America and the besieged island, bringing a new definition to the concept of war reporting, focussing not on soldiers but on civilians, his 'unsung heroes' … Those black-faced men with bloodshot eyes … fighting fires … the girls who cradled the steering wheel of a heavy ambulance in their*

---

[6] H. Cudlipp, *The Prerogative of the Harlot* (1980), 34.
[7] Hamilton, *Journalism's Roving Eye* (2009), 194.
[8] Gellhorn, *The View from the Ground* (1989), 70.

arms. The policeman who stands guard over that unexploded bomb. 'These things must be seen' he kept insisting.[9]

Foreign reporting in the 1930s and 1940s, like Gellhorn's, Murrow's, or the descriptions of the discovery of the German concentration camps from reporters like Richard Dimbleby, offered a narrative of conscience, a focus on victims and the humanitarian consequences of big events which still informs much international reporting today. They consolidated in the minds of editors and readers the core importance of bearing witness to unfurling events. A concern with human rights and humanitarian issues remains a feature of Anglo-American foreign journalism but is less true of coverage generated by other countries.

Following the Second World War, it was the Cold War which defined international reporting, from Korea, through Vietnam and into the 1980s. The resources news organisations devoted to international news reflected the politics of the time, with major bureaux in Moscow, Eastern Europe and Asia, and teams deployed to cover the proxy conflicts generated by the Cold War, in Africa, Central America and elsewhere.

However, by the late 1980s a number of factors coincided to reshape the provision of international news significantly. The fall of the Berlin Wall in 1989, which allowed the era of globalisation to develop, broadly coincided with the 'corporatisation' of news media and a renewed focus on costs and value, particularly in the USA. At the same time, cable, satellite and later the internet delivered real-time 24-hour news – revolutionising news production and distribution. The coincidence of these three factors – globalisation, economics and technology – over a 20-year period has brought swift and far-reaching change into the heart of journalism and particularly the reporting of international news.

The end of the Cold War fragmented the political lens through which much of the world had until then been viewed by Western news organisations – still the biggest, best resourced and most influential news sources. As one *New York Times* editor wrote in an internal memo:

We can be less preoccupied with the daily official rhetoric from the capitals ... Our report should reflect more fully the social, cultural, intellectual, scientific and technological revolutions which, more than the political, are transforming the world society.[10]

---

[9] Sperber, *Murrow: His Life and Times* (1986), 179.
[10] Seymour Topping quoted in Hamilton, *Journalism's Roving Eye*, 462.

1989 brought many predictions of the kind of world that would follow – from a 'New World Order' (George Bush), the 'End of History' (Francis Fukuyama) to the 'Clash of Civilisations' (Samuel Huntingdon). What predominantly followed was a freeing up and deregulating of previously closed or restricted economic markets which ushered in the age of globalisation. Easier global trading combined with global communications and the ease and falling costs of air travel meant the world was more interconnected than ever.

In terms of the news agenda, and in the style and tone news was reported, a 'dispatch from abroad' began to feel dated and less relevant. An increasingly interconnected world demanded a similarly connected and contextualised form of journalism. Specialist subject correspondents supplemented by 'firemen' reporters who flew in and flew out to address moments of crisis or acute interest – and whose celebrity grew as a consequence – became increasingly established as the model for reporting the world as the numbers of bureaux and foreign correspondents shrank.

The international news agenda continued to be dominated by major events however. The first Gulf War, a civil war on the European mainland as Yugoslavia fell apart, followed by the horrific events of 9/11 and two major military campaigns in Iraq and Afghanistan, put more strain on foreign news budgets.

The advent of 24-hour news had greatly accelerated the news cycle, starting to redefine the work of the international reporter. CNN launched in 1980 and five years later CNN International, the global service, launched. The impact of live TV coverage of events like the Challenger Space Shuttle disaster and, in 1991, the start of the first Gulf War gave a new imperative to live reporting – and saw the launch of hundreds of competing 24-hour channels over the next few years. The speed of the news cycle was accelerated further with the advent of news services on the internet 15 years later.

Rather than the considered journalism for an era of print deadlines and broadcast bulletins, news was now 'always on', with services in constant need of being fed and updated. As digital technology took hold, many kinds of organisation were able to pass information around the world in real time – the benefits weren't restricted to news operations. Charlie Beckett, the Director of Polis at LSE explains it like this:

> We forget that we're in a situation with enormous flows of information globally – finance, business, diplomacy – lots of information digitally zooming about that isn't connected to journalism. So the primary importance of reportage is less.[11]

---

[11] Interview with author, Feb. 2010.

For decades, foreign correspondents had fulfilled the dual role of reporting news of interest to their audiences at home and analysing and commenting on those events in a way which gave their organisation a distinct point of view. They had enjoyed the position of being the principal source of information from far-flung lands. More than that, through eyewitness reporting, they served a public purpose in bearing witness to major events.

The acceleration of the news cycle and the arrival of digital technology started to challenge the routines and exclusivity of international reporting. The information revolution devalued the currency of mainstream foreign news. The premium or value in news became in up-to-the-minute breaking news supplemented with comment and analysis for specialist or niche audiences. As Reuters Editor-in-Chief David Schlesinger puts it, the value of news is like a dumbbell – with the weight at either end, and not much in the middle. [12] The 'middle' was perhaps where most bureaux correspondents had plied their trade. Sometimes breaking major news, sometimes providing deep analysis, but for the main part filing features or daily reports that were neither. This basic news became commoditised as news output increased exponentially with 24-hour channels and the internet.

As the internet brought down the geographical boundaries to accessing news, agendas started to change as well. Different audiences in different countries have always perceived events in different ways. Suddenly they were able to see across the fence to how others were reporting the news. This started to affect agendas – either by strengthening national perspectives through shrill opinion or, in contrast, by opening up a more global approach to issues as news organisations found new markets overseas.[13]

News now appears to be ubiquitous and ambient, with the premium on speed and comment – neither of which necessarily require expensive bureaux. Emily Bell, the former Digital Director of the *Guardian,* recalls that when she and the paper's Foreign Editor, Harriet Sherwood, were in Washington when news of the Fort Hood shootings[14] broke in 2009, each did what their roles dictated. The Foreign Editor hit the phones, deployed a correspondent, fixed air tickets and hotel rooms. The Digital Editor went to the web. They had a moment of realisation. The immediate facts of the story would be known and the events over before their reporter arrived. But moment-by-moment updates were available from the emergency services on the web. In terms of breaking news, the web won hands down over old-fashioned reporter-led newsgathering. There was still value in sending a reporter – to provide

[12] Interview with author, July 2010.
[13] More people in the US now read the *Guardian*, a British newspaper, than read the *LA Times*. More than half the users of the BBC News website live outside the UK.
[14] The Fort Hood shootings was a mass shooting that took place on 5 Nov. 2009, at Fort Hood—the most populous US military base in the world, located just outside Killeen, TX—in which a gunman killed 13 people and wounded 30 others.

background, feature coverage and analysis, but not in the traditional sense of finding out what had happened on a fast-breaking story.[15]

This shift in value changed what was expected of a foreign correspondent. Productivity had to rise to meet the new demands; there was an even greater imperative to cut costs, and the editorial focus switched to immediacy over general interest, with serious news organisations attempting to supplement and perhaps compensate with comment and analysis at the other end of the scale.

The renewed and relentless focus on costs was partly driven by new corporate ownership seeking to deliver value to shareholders, exacerbated by economic recession and the erosion of the traditional advertising revenues as audiences fragmented across satellite, cable and internet services. All news organisations began to look at how they could find the money to invest in new digital services. And at the forefront of concerns about costs was expensive international news.

This rapid overview of the evolution of international news and the foreign correspondent is merely intended to illustrate how the combination of *economics* in the news industry, new *technology* and *globalisation* accelerated change over a 20-year period and has fundamentally altered the structures of international news coverage established over the previous 120 years. And those structural changes have affected what we learn of the world, and how.

Let's consider each of those factors in turn.

---

[15] Interview with author, Oct. 2009.

2. Economics

Although the impact of reducing budgets on Western news organisations, and on international coverage in particular, are much discussed there is no single quantitative study which analyses the reduction in bureaux and coverage over the past decades. However, the general narrative is not in dispute. As Andrew Currah points out, 'no matter how powerful the philanthropic spirit or quest for power, the practical costs of journalism demand a robust economic model (which is looking increasingly unstable in the present context)'.[16]

The economic model has been under strain for some years. Seymour Topping, former Managing Editor of the *New York Times*, noted in the 1990s, 'The great threat to intelligent coverage of foreign news is not so much a lack of interest as it is a concentration of ownership that is profit-driven and a lack of inclination to meet responsibilities except that of the bottom line.'[17] As new corporate owners took hold of both broadcast and print news organisations in the 1980s and 1990s they demanded that journalism paid its way. The paternalistic arguments of public interest, or magnates' desires for political influence, largely gave way to the requirements of shareholders. This pressure was exacerbated by economic downturns, and the spiralling capital costs of printing plant, digital newsrooms and satellite-enabled broadcasting facilities. In addition, advertising revenues were undercut by the fragmentation of media, with the growth of cable and satellite services and the internet.

Journalism met the market – and found it uncomfortable. Old hands often ascribe malign motives to those whose responsibility was to reconcile editorial aspirations with the bottom line. The truth, that expensive journalism seldom paid its way, was being exposed.

International reporting, with its high costs, was often at the forefront of budget cuts necessitated by these changes. Former correspondent Jill Carroll, in a study for Harvard's Shorenstein Center, estimated in 2007 that small US

---

[16] Currah, *What's Happening to Our News* (2008), 20.
[17] Quoted in James Hoge, 'Foreign News: Who Gives a Damn', *Columbia Journalism Review* (1997), 48.

newspapers had shrunk their foreign bureaux by 30 per cent and large papers by 10 per cent since 2000, contributing to a fall in international coverage.[18]

She quotes the Project for Excellence in Journalism (PEJ) Study which showed that front-page coverage of foreign affairs in US newspapers had halved between 1987 and 2004[19] – although broadcast coverage had risen since the 9/11 attacks and remained higher than pre-2001 levels, principally driven by reporting from Afghanistan and Iraq. The 2004 Pew study found that front-page stories about foreign affairs accounted for 'the lowest total in any year we have ever studied'.

But Carroll argues there is a public appetite as well as a public need for international news and that it can be profitable – citing the success of magazines like *The Economist*.

> *Insightful, well-informed foreign reporting is essential to keeping the national debate vigorous and churning. This moral argument won't hold sway in many boardrooms, but the financial incentives to produce good quality foreign news should. Hopefully financial decision makers will have the foresight to realise they are drastically undervaluing foreign news coverage and have the wisdom to hang onto and invest in this valuable asset.*

There is little evidence however, outside of niche publications and services, that foreign news drives profit. And certainly the publishers and broadcasters have failed to exploit any such 'undervaluation', particularly when it can cost upwards of $250,000 p.a. to maintain an overseas bureau (and significantly more in places like Iraq or Afghanistan).

Overseas offices are inevitably expensive. Among the costs are not just rent and salaries, but overseas allowances, support for the correspondent's family like school fees and housing rent allowances, the costs of local operations and staff, transmission, security (depending on location) and more, which all contribute to significant overheads. The revenue directly generated by international news (advertising on the foreign pages for example) has never been sufficient to cover these costs. They have always been subsidised by profits generated from other parts of the newspaper or news network – sports, business or classified advertising.

Now, newspapers – and increasingly broadcasting – have lost their role as market intermediaries. Readers and viewers no longer need classified or display ads to buy the goods and services they need – Craigslist, eBay and

---

[18] Jill Carroll, 'Foreign News Coverage: The US Media's Undervalued Asset', Joan Shorenstein Center, Harvard, March 2007.
[19] PEJ *State of the News Media* (2006).

many other sites provide that access essentially for free. Where advertising once supported the costs of news production, the internet has pulled that support away, as James Fallows of *The Atlantic* magazine points out:

> *The Internet has been one giant system for stripping away such cross-subsidies. Why look to the newspaper real-estate listings when you can get more up-to-date, searchable info on Zillow – or better travel deals on Orbitz, or a broader range of movie showtimes on Yahoo? Google has been the most powerful unbundling agent of all. It lets users find the one article they are looking for, rather than making them buy the entire paper that paid the reporter. It lets advertisers reach the one customer who is searching for their product, rather than making them advertise to an entire class of readers.*[20]

McKinsey have estimated that more than half the forecast growth in global internet advertising will be a reallocation of advertising spend from elsewhere.[21] This shift in spend has disrupted the business plans of most traditional media organisations. The loss of advertising meant many news organisations have concentrated their resources close to home – with international coverage being the sacrifice made.

But the pressures on costs pre-date the internet. In 1987 CBS News announced what was then the biggest cutback in its history: $33 million cut from its budget, staff cut by 15 per cent and a series of major bureau closures. As CBS employees Richard Cohen and Dan Rather wrote in the *New York Times*:

> *CBS Inc is a profitable valuable Fortune 500 corporation whose stock is setting new records. But 215 people lost their jobs so that the stockholders would have even more money in their pockets. More profits. That's what business is about.*[22]

In the 1980s, American TV networks each maintained about 15 foreign bureaux; today they have six or fewer. ABC shut down its offices in Moscow, Paris and Tokyo; NBC closed bureaux in Beijing, Cairo and Johannesburg. Aside from a one-person ABC bureau in Nairobi, there were no network bureaux left at all in Africa, India or South America.[23]

It was a cold shower for those used to the warm bath of patronage and

---

[20] www.theatlantic.com/magazine/print/2010/05/how-to-save-the-news/8095/.
[21] Currah, *What's Happening*, 38.
[22] Peter J. Boyer, *Who Killed CBS News?* (Random House, 1988), 331.
[23] 'Demise of the Foreign Correspondent', *Washington Post*, 18 Feb. 2007.

subsidy. The changes inevitably had an impact on the range and tone of what was reported. Advertisers wanted viewers, and viewers wanted something more accessible and entertaining, more directly relevant to their lives, than news from a far-off land.

Rebecca MacKinnon, a former CNN Bureau Chief in Beijing, can trace the path of retreat.

> *When I first joined in 1992 what appeared on air was driven by the International Desk who would tell the shows what was on offer. In 1995 CNN and Time Warner merged and a cultural shift began where there was more emphasis on the ratings and the Time Warner share price. Glitzy magazine shows came in and the production side had more say in what international news was commissioned. Then after the AOL merger in 2000, the dot.com bubble burst, the share price dropped and the decision making moved firmly to the prime time shows. Whether a correspondent could go anywhere was contingent on domestic news interest. It got to the point in 2003 where I was told my expertise was getting in the way of the coverage they wanted.*[24]

She left shortly afterwards.

Many in the profession believe there is a high cultural and social price to be paid for this retreat from international news. Fewer bureaux and correspondents means less international reporting on screen or in the paper. *Washington Post* correspondent Pamela Constable itemised the impact in 2007:

> *Today, Americans' need to understand the struggles of distant peoples is greater than ever. Our troops are fighting in Iraq and Afghanistan, countries that we did not know enough about when we invaded them and that we are still trying to fathom. We have been victimized by foreign terrorists, yet we still cannot imagine why anyone would hate us. Our economy is intimately linked to global markets, our population is nearly 20 percent foreign-born, and our lives are directly affected by borderless scourges such as global warming and AIDS. Knowing about the world is not a luxury; it is an urgent necessity. But instead of stepping up coverage of international affairs, American newspapers and television networks are steadily cutting back.*[25]

---

[24] Interview with author.
[25] Ibid.

According to the US broadcast news analyst Andrew Tyndall, the three US network news programmes reported an average of 1,500 minutes of news each year from foreign bureaux in 1989, which had halved by 2009.[26] Even allowing for the momentous events of 20 years ago, it is a significant drop.

Ethan Zuckerman, from the Berkman Center at Harvard, told the 2010 TED Global conference:

> *The world is getting more global and connected. More problems are global, economics are global in scale but our media is getting less global by the day. If you watched a US nightly news broadcast in the 1970's on average 35% would be international news. In the 2000's it's down to 12–15%.*[27]

Many news organisations hit a downward spiral following the arrival of satellite and cable and, later, the internet. Their readerships or audiences fell in the face of increased competition, leading to reduced revenues and the need for more efficiencies and cuts, thinning their content and risking further falls in consumption.[28]

It is a picture repeated elsewhere. A recent OECD study on news estimates that newspapers in 20 out of 31 OECD countries face declining readerships with significant decreases in many.

> *The economic crisis and the fall in offline and online advertising spending in general have created additional problems for most newspapers leading to large falls in their advertising revenues, loss of circulation, the closure of newspapers and shedding of newsroom staff in many OECD countries.*[29]

In Britain, as elsewhere, international coverage has suffered as a consequence. Research by the Media Standards Trust has shown the decline in international coverage in print in the UK.

> *Based on our content analysis, there were nearly 40% fewer international stories across the four newspapers we studied in 2009 compared to 1979. As a proportion of these print*

---

[26] Tyndall Report: http://tyndallreport.com/yearinreview2009/foreignbureaus/
[27] www.ted.com/talks/ethan_zuckerman.html.
[28] However the volume of foreign news in US newspapers was never high. Woodward's study in 1927 (*Foreign News in American Morning Newspapers*, Columbia University Press, 1930), showed foreign news occupied on average no more than 5% of the sample newspapers editorial space outside of times of crisis. This figure has proved robust in the years since – although rising during years of international turmoil.
[29] OECD Working Party on the Information Economy, *The Evolution of News and the Internet* (June 2010).

> *papers, the percentage of international news dropped over the*
> *same period from 20% to 11%.[30]*

A study of UK television found that in 2007 the international factual output of the four main terrestrial channels was the lowest on record as such coverage was pushed towards the minority digital channels.[31]

A more recent study for Oxfam, the International Broadcasting Trust and Polis found the position in British broadcasting was healthier than in newspapers – but dominated by the publicly funded BBC which had about 200 foreign correspondents plus freelancers and stringers. The BBC and Channel 4 have maintained their international coverage despite economic and structural pressures. International coverage at ITV, however, dropped by 73 per cent between 2007 and 2009 (there are no figures for the number of foreign correspondents at the station). Channel 5 coverage has also dropped, but not as drastically. Sky News has between 9 and 11 foreign-based correspondents.[32]

The report argues that decisive action is needed to counter the unplanned and undesired effects of these changes.

> *Without urgent action, there is a very real threat that the*
> *international agenda could fade from our mainstream*
> *channels. This future is not the outcome of design or a result*
> *of malicious intent but benign apathy as those that should*
> *champion it stay quiet.*

While there has been hand-wringing among many journalism professionals about this contraction, with an accompanying lament about the social impact of less foreign news, the changes have largely been met with apathy by the public. They've been happy to enjoy the increased media choice technology has brought without worrying about sacrifices made along the way.

Perhaps they recognise that there is another perspective on this tale of cuts and retrenchment. Not least, that there was much waste and extravagance at the height of the era of foreign bureau reporting and a flushing out of high cost and inefficiency was both inevitable and healthy. Andrew Lack, President of NBC News in the 1990s, explains:

> *The dirty little secret … was that those people were not very*
> *productive. I was at the old CBS Paris bureau and the old*

---

[30] Media Standards Trust, *Shrinking World?* (Oct. 2010).
[31] www.dfid.gov.uk/pubs/files/screeningreport-020608.pdf.
[32] Phil Harding, 'The Great Global Switch Off': www.oxfam.org.uk/resources/papers/downloads/great_global_switch_off.pdf.

CBS London bureau and there were an awful lot of guys
sitting around and going to Savile Row and buying fancy-
looking suits ... There was a noblesse oblige in the bureaux
system that was a waste of money, and bullshit ... that level
of waste was pulled out of the system.[33]

Paul Friedman, CBS News VP, also saw it as an issue of basic efficiency: 'You spend $4million a year to maintain a bureau that does no work and then works like hell for three weeks.'

In 2006 NBC News cut a further 300 people from its newsgathering staff to invest in digital services. As one business commentator noted: 'Given the competitive landscape, a drastic change is necessary for these operations.'[34] No one could afford foreign resources sitting idle while cost pressures mounted, competition increased and there was a growing imperative to invest in new digital services and technology. And in any case, the old news promotion 'Give us twenty minutes and we'll give you the world' had always been a myth.

In many cases there simply wasn't sufficient justification for a network of bureaux in the first place. Marcus Brauchli, Executive Editor of the *Washington Post*, explains:

Foreign Bureaux are non-essential for a lot of papers that
previously had them. When they had large profit margins
they maintained bureaux in places where it was not essential
in order to be seen as 'players' but it didn't serve the interests
of their readers any better than taking the AP. For the LA
Times to have correspondents in Mexico, Rio or the Pacific
Rim makes sense, but perhaps not across Europe and the
Middle East.[35]

He said while the *New York Times* could justifiably call itself a global paper, and the *Washington Post*, read by US policy-makers, could justify covering US activities in distant corners of the globe, it made no sense for the *Detroit News* or the *Miami Herald* to try to have correspondents everywhere. They could in any case rely on news agencies like Reuters and the AP which were established to provide international coverage and spread the cost among subscribers.

As Paul Slavin, a former Executive Producer at ABC World News, said, asking questions about foreign bureaux is 'like someone asking "Why don't we still use clay tablets?" ... It's a whole different world now.'[36] Bureaux

---

[33] Downie and Kaiser, *The News about the News*, 151.
[34] 'NBC Says Viewers Won't Notice Cuts in News Staff', *New York Times*, 20 Oct. 2006.
[35] Interview with author, Feb. 2010.
[36] 'Bureau of Missing Bureaus', *American Journalism Review* (Nov. 2003): www.ajr.org.

began as major news embassies in countries where news was likely to be found – Moscow, Israel, Japan, South Africa. As the efficiencies took hold the structure evolved into something more like the hub and spoke structure used by airlines, where bureaux were jumping-off points for other parts of the world. Now, with digital technology, even the hub and spoke structure is giving way to a more fluid approach to covering the news, relying more on parachute journalism, stringers and freelances.

Costs were cut to invest in digital technology. New equipment provided speed and flexibility. ABC News President David Westin explained it starkly: 'Technology now makes it possible to have bureaux without a receptionist, three edit suites and studio cameras.'[37] His former colleague, Chuck Lustig, put it like this:

> *We can cover more with less people as the equipment has shrunk to the point where a single journalist can carry on their back everything they need to shoot, edit and transmit their story. The Foreign Correspondent has become a simple fireman who goes from fire to fire just like the neighbourhood fire brigade. Once the fire is out they move on ...*[38]

Fireman or parachute journalism is generally used as a pejorative phrase indicating a lack of commitment on the part of whoever deploys in such a fashion. This view is summarised by Philip Seib, Professor of Journalism at the University of Southern California:

> *The parachute approach often produces news without context: the war or other humanitarian emergency appears to news consumers to have suddenly exploded, a distortion that occurs because journalists have not been on the scene to cover the situation while the fuse was burning ... this kind of journalism is intrinsically misleading.*[39]

Yet most traditional foreign correspondents are to some degree parachutists. Henry Stanley was when he found Dr Livingstone. And it is not unusual for bureau correspondents to travel extensively away from their base.

It is a means of editors getting better value foreign coverage by moving money out of fixed-cost bureaux into the variable budgets of reactive coverage. It allows more correspondents on the ground, and helps to develop their reporting skills. In terms of quantity and diversity of output, digital

---

[37] www.reuters.com/article/idUSN0344510720071005.
[38] Interview with author, Feb. 2010.
[39] Perlmutter and Hamilton, *From Pigeons to News Portals* (2007),161.

technology made parachute journalism efficient in a way fixed bureaux were not.

It can have editorial advantages as well. Philip Gourevitch, based in the USA, has been travelling to Africa for 15 years to report for *The New Yorker*.

> *It forces me to constantly reboot my perspective. I go in, I go deep, I get into the fine grain insider perspective of Rwandan experience, then I come home and have to translate that and to see what the larger shapes are that travel well and have meaning to a larger outside audience as well as to Rwandans. When you arrive somewhere foreign you notice everything. When you live there a while and it ceases to become foreign you stop noticing things that you still should notice as a reporter. Going in and out is a safeguard against that.*[40]

Once in the field, reporters can now do more than ever before. Marcus Wilford was ABC's bureau chief in London responsible for covering Europe, the Middle East and Africa.

> *ABC experimented two years ago by opening 7 new international bureaux – these were small one person so-called digital operations. The idea was that with a lightweight camera that was easy to use, and other handheld technology, plus a high speed internet connection in their homes to feed from – we could field reporters all over the world for a relatively low cost.*[41]

My own experience at the BBC mirrors this. As a field producer in the 1980s, satellite dishes had to be flown in, often on chartered aircraft, to allow our reporters to broadcast live or to send reports back to London. By the 1990s, dishes could be put into trucks or broken down into a series of portable boxes. Within the last two years, BBC teams were broadcasting live from the Indian elections with a mobile phone and a laptop.

The adoption of new technology has been driven by the dual imperatives of cutting costs and increasing productivity. Speed and flexibility in reporting are not the only opportunities in the new digital landscape. The internet allows new services to launch at relatively low cost, which can supplement and enhance core news operations and provide new economic models. The high fixed costs of newspaper production (raw materials, printing presses,

[40] Interview with author, Sept. 2010.
[41] Interview with author, Feb. 2010.

distribution) make them less agile than broadcasters or agencies in adopting new models, with occasional exceptions.

As the old economic models have broken down, new ones are emerging. These encompass new forms of subsidy, non-profit and state funding and basic entrepreneurialism.

New forms of subsidy

Some larger specialist news organisations have found success by striking the right cross-subsidy balance between immediate breaking news, or consumer-focused content, and in-depth analysis for which high subscriptions can be charged.

As Chrystia Freeland put it in the *Columbia Journalism Review*:

> *Their challenge is to determine the right mix of professional content, which is sold to a relatively small client base, usually bundled with data, for extremely high rates and consumer content which brings in less money but reaches a bigger audience.*[42]

She cites as examples the specialist services offered by Bloomberg, the *FT* and Thomson Reuters.

Bloomberg, a business built around financial terminals and the global trade in financial information, has pushed aggressively into the consumer news space – including in print with its acquisition of *Business Week*. Matt Winkler, the Founding Editor of Bloomberg News explained:

> *The virtue of radio, TV, the web and magazines is that they increase the awareness of the value of Bloomberg ... There are plenty of experts in all sorts of fields around the world who might not have a Bloomberg (terminal). But they become aware of Bloomberg because of a story on our website or TV. That expert then decides to talk to that journalist and as a result the Bloomberg terminal becomes more valuable.*[43]

Building a consumer brand in order to drive more value into niche subscription products seems to be a successful strategy for some global players, particularly in the financial sector where they can command significant subscriptions for specialist information. John Ridding, CEO of the *FT*, says:

---

[42] C. J. R. Freeland, 'The Rise of Private News', *Columbia Journalism Review* (July 2010).
[43] Ibid.

> *The traditional FT newspaper and FT.Com are at the centre*
> *of an umbrella around which we are developing even more*
> *speciality and niche publications. They can be organic*
> *like China Confidential (edited by a former FT Beijing*
> *Bureau Chief) or they can be acquisitions like Medley (a*
> *high-end professional analysis service) on Money Media*
> *(an aggregation and reporting service aimed at managers).*
> *These niches, drawing on the value of the brand and their*
> *infrastructure, can be extremely profitable. If you go from the*
> *newsstand to Medley there's quite a difference in price!*[44]

Thomson Reuters were among the first to straddle the high-value niche service and consumer content and continue to do so. For example, new services like the video portal 'Reuters Insider' – a web-based video service offering streams of information produced by the company's reporters together with 150 other partners. It is a broadband interactive platform which targets Thomson Reuters' existing 500,000 clients worldwide. It has been described as YouTube for the financially interested. Subscribers navigate by sector, date, markets, or region, or apply filters to create their own personalised channels.

On one day (20 July 2010) content included video analysis from Reuters experts, but also raw video from partners on subjects like trends in Chinese gaming communities, top global football stars, one-minute headlines on CSR news, business school 'knowledgecasts', and fashion, technology and lifestyle videos. The partners gain additional distribution, Reuters gains additional content, enriching the service.

For news organisations seeking to find a commercial model to support international operations there may be lessons here. Three of the more successful news organisations, maintaining strength in international reporting, are doing so by leveraging their consumer brand to derive additional value from niche subscribers. And they have worked out the relationship between the value of fast-breaking news and the value of in-depth analysis that they offer. They are specialist providers, but understanding how low-value, high-reach consumer news and high-value, low-reach specialist news can support each other is clearly one route to sustainable global operations.

The model is a new variant on what has always happened – subsidising expensive international operations (which build brand and reputation) from more profitable areas of activity. They are not the only ones experimenting.

[44] Ibid.

Entrepreneurialism

As traditional news magazines like *Newsweek* and *Time* struggled financially, *Monocle* magazine was launched with a small subscriber base but an ambitious niche foreign agenda. Launched in 2007 as an expensive print magazine and website it sets out to offer a global briefing on international affairs, business, culture and design. At a time when competitors were closing overseas operations, *Monocle* launched with permanent bureaux in Tokyo, Zurich and New York, and now Hong Kong. Publisher Tyler Brûlé says the cuts elsewhere in international coverage provided a market opportunity for his magazine:

> We had the sense that cutbacks at various newspaper and
> broadcast outlets meant the diversity of international news
> was narrowing. What we were witnessing was the rise of
> wire service use and a same-ness in international pages – the
> same ten stories everywhere. Five years later, despite the rise
> of more blog and comment, we haven't seen a rise in more
> original reporting. I'd argue there's less.

He believes the fixed bureaux are an important contributor to economic success – because of the way they relate to retail and other commercial extensions of the specialist *Monocle* brand:

> Having bureaux shows commitment and also muscle.
> In Hong Kong we're experimenting with a hybrid model
> that has a shop-front and awning at street level (a big
> Monocle sign in a hot HK retail district works 24 hours as a
> billboard) and a bureau in the back. The retail activity pays
> for the real estate and this allows us to have a proper set
> up (full communications, desks, meeting facilities) for our
> correspondent and researcher. Moreover, they don't man the
> shop as there's a separate team for that. This is working so
> well that we're looking to replicate this model in Sao Paulo
> and Sydney in 2011.[45]

Last year, he adds, revenues rose by 30 per cent and the company moved into profit ahead of schedule. The magazine has 15,000 global subscribers, who pay a flat rate of £75, a premium on the £5 cover price, whatever their location.

The same principle is at work in new online news services too, as the *New York Times* recently reported:

---

[45] Interview with author, July 2010.

*Many other publications, confronted with the painful
math, have reached the same conclusion: the business
needs alternate schemes of support. Some have adapted
tried-and-true formulas. The Daily Beast is backed by a
generous billionaire, Barry Diller; others are mimicking
NPR's nonprofit model; Politico makes the majority of its
revenue from, of all things, advertising in an offshoot print
newspaper.*[46]

The article profiles Sam Apple's attempts to launch an online journal, *The Faster Times*, and his calculation that the cost of a single article was approximately £10. With the addition of international newsgathering costs, and content less attractive to domestic advertisers, the cost of foreign news is probably higher than that per item – so it becomes easy to see how maintaining offices around the world becomes uneconomic.

Non-profit and state funding

Finding ways to subsidise or underwrite the costs of foreign reporting, to support its value to the news organisation's brand, appears to be the only sustainable model.

In the UK, the *Guardian*, which maintains a spread of international coverage as well as investing in digital operations, is loss-making but supported by the Scott Trust from the profits of other publications. Sky News in the UK is a loss-leader, supported by the profits of other Sky channels because of the profile and prestige it brings to the network. News Corporation's News Division (publishing *The Times* and the *Wall St Journal* among others) contributes only about 20 per cent of its parent company's revenues. Its diversified interests in cable, satellite and film can offset any print losses.

The BBC, like some other public service broadcasters, has maintained a wide spread of international bureaux and coverage thanks to public funding. During the 1990s as other networks were cutting back, the BBC took a deliberate decision to invest in international newsgathering as a means of providing a differentiated public value out of its licence-fee funding.

State funding has led to a rise in global news services across Europe, the Middle East, Asia and Latin America – none of them commercially profitable in their own right. The willingness of other countries to subsidise international services was something from which the President of Columbia University, Lee Bollinger recently urged the American government to learn when he called for greater public funding:

---

[46] 'Putting a Price on Words', *New York Times*, 10 May 2010.

> We should think about American journalism as a mixed
> system, where the mission is to get the balance right. To
> me a key priority is to strengthen our public broadcasting
> role in the global arena. In today's rapidly globalising and
> interconnected world, other countries are developing a strong
> media presence. In addition to the BBC, there is China's
> CCTV and Xinhua news, as well as Qatar's Al Jazeera.[47]

There is currently a strong debate in the USA and elsewhere about the desirability of public subsidy for news.[48] The OECD reports that

> some countries (e.g. France, Netherlands, Sweden) have put
> emergency measures in place to financially help the struggling
> newspaper industry. Calls for such assistance have been
> issued by the newspaper sectors in countries such as Italy
> and Spain … More generally, the question of what potential
> roles government support might take in preserving a diverse
> and local press without putting the independence of the press
> at stake … is being debated. The question is also whether
> and how the production of high-quality and pluralistic news
> content can be left to the market alone.[49]

There is no question that public broadcasters have managed to maintain a stronger international presence than their commercial rivals. The BBC, Deutsche Welle and NPR in the US all have strong international operations thanks to public funding and have maintained the traditions of international reporting. However state funding does not necessarily support a plurality of news provision either and, in many circumstances, runs significant risks of compromising the independence of the news media. Alternative approaches to sustainable international reporting have to be (and are being) developed.

Not least, at an individual, correspondent level – Robin Allbritton was a former AP and *New York Daily News* reporter:

> In March 2003, I made it (to Iraq), becoming the Web's first
> fully reader-funded journalist-blogger. With the support of
> thousands of readers, we raised almost $15,000. … It was
> one of the moments in journalism when everything worked.
> It was a grand, and successful, experiment in independent

---

[47] Lee Bollinger, 'Journalism Needs Government Help', *Wall St Journal*, 14 July 2010: http://online.wsj.com/article/SB10001424052748704629804575324782605510168.html.
[48] www.cjr.org/reconstruction/the_reconstruction_of_american.php.
[49] OECD.

journalism. In 2004, I moved to Iraq, where I would spend the next two years. It was a raucous, scary and exciting place with a lot of news going on. But I've since moved on to Beirut and the wider region. I now report for a variety of outlets.[50]

David Axe, a freelance reporter working from the USA, does something similar with the War is Boring blog.[51] He highlights issues he would like to report and appeals for reader donations to help fund his trips, including those to Iraq, Lebanon, Japan, East Timor, Afghanistan, Somalia, Chad, Nicaragua, Kenya, Gabon and other countries.

In the USA organisations like the Deer Creek Foundation in St Louis, or the Pulitzer Center of Crisis Reporting, support international reporting with grants to individual journalists to report specific issues. The pressures on corporate newsgathering have helped spawn innovation at an individual level.

Conclusion

- From the 1980s onwards there has been a relentless paring back of international resources by Western news organisations in the face of budget cuts forced by declining revenues, the need for investment in digital technology and the demands of corporate shareholders.

- The market has exposed traditional cross-subsidies of high-cost foreign reporting. Some organisations were caught in a downward spiral of cutting editorial budgets, falling audiences, and reduced revenue, leading to further cuts.

- The 'middle' has fallen out of the news market, with value increasingly polarised in immediacy and breaking news or in-depth and specialist analysis.

- However within this context there has also been innovation. Budgets have been rebalanced from the fixed costs of bureaux to more variable and fluid costs of reactive coverage.

- New kinds of cross-subsidy for international coverage are emerging, there is grassroots entrepreneurialism from individual reporters and a renewed focus on non-profit and state funding for international news.

[50] www.back-to-iraq.com/about
[51] www.warisboring.com/

3. Technology

It is a paradox that as the traditional foreign news bureaux have shrunk, the opportunities to find out about the world have greatly increased. The change reflects a structural shift in news provision, with foreign reporting at the forefront. As old models of international newsgathering suffered, new models have been spawned – although not always swiftly adopted by what are now called 'legacy media'.

News organisations have taken themselves online – some profitably, most not – in competition with aggregators, blogs and digital services from a wide range of organisations and individuals. Technology is changing how we obtain information – mobile phones, RSS feeds, blog aggregators, search engines all provide a greater depth and range of information than was possible 10 years ago. The social media phenomenon has turned the 140 characters of Twitter into an effective news source. We are increasingly guided by our friends and peers through recommendation and links. Everybody now has access to the public space, giving rise to citizen journalism and more.

It is not simply as a platform for news organisations that the internet has had an impact on how we learn about the world. As all organisations move online – as well as individuals through social media – newsgathering has been transformed.

All technological advances in reporting are designed either to transmit information about an event closer to the time it actually occurred or to get journalists closer to the event. In the 2003 Iraq war there was live satellite reporting from battles on the frontline for the first time. Internet and mobile technology will make that even easier in future.

As Andrew Marr noted in his book *My Trade*, the history of foreign reporting has been the history of changing technology as well.

> *Transatlantic cables, airmail, wired photographs from the front. … there has always been a new development to exploit. The Second World War was the first radio war,*

> *with correspondents sending back vivid sound despatches;*
> *Korea saw the arrival of lightweight cameras and television*
> *footage from the front line; by Vietnam there was colour.*
> *The two Gulf wars were widely described as video-arcade*
> *conflicts because of the eerie green footage of missiles homing*
> *in and obliterating targets. The modern impact of satellites,*
> *electronic news gathering, sat-phones and digital*
> *cameras ...*[52]

He suggests this technological development cuts two ways. On the one hand it has brought speed and vividness. On the other, it has cut back the time a reporter has to watch, think, listen and compose. Where once a correspondent might be able to operate almost independently of the newsdesk, now the arrival of 24-hour news means they are shackled to the demands of the output hour by hour. For many, it raises the spectre of considered journalism being swamped by the needs of continuous news.

As Kate Adie, the former BBC correspondent, wrote in her memoirs:

> *Increasingly hacks were tethered to the satellite dish, always*
> *on hand to deliver the 'live spot', in a curious belief that*
> *rabbiting on live is a more relevant and informed kind of*
> *reporting; in reality, someone stuck next to a dish for hours*
> *on end is the last creature on earth to have learned anything*
> *new, and probably unaware of a corpse twenty yards away.*[53]

In truth there now had to be two kinds of reporting – live reporting for the news channels and the web and more traditional dispatches for the morning edition or the evening bulletin – distinct servicing of the two ends of the news value chain. The challenge for news organisations has been in preventing newsgathering operations from being overwhelmed by the demands of new platforms and preserving resources for original journalism.

Technology has unquestionably made foreign reporting more productive – in terms of quantity at least. Today, armed with mobile phone and laptop, a reporter can file live from almost anywhere on the planet. As well as cutting newsgathering costs for established media, technology has breathed fresh life into freelance journalism. Now independent journalists are no longer dependent on newspapers and channels to reach the public. They can leapfrog over the heads of editors and report directly.

This has led to a rise in freelance reporting, from local journalists, stringers

---

[52] Marr, *My Trade* (2004), 332.
[53] Adie, *The Kindness of Strangers* (2002), 355.

and those unable to get, or uninterested in, staff jobs, setting up their own news sites and operations. For example, Graham Holliday is a freelance journalist living in Kigali who runs Kigaliwire.com, a blog and aggregation site for news about Rwanda. It doesn't pay, but he manages to support it through other work that the profile of the site brings in. His coverage rests on technical knowledge and an understanding of how social media works. 'I can report with a camera, a £5 a month Pay-As-You-Go phone and a £45 web template. I can file to 45 or more sites automatically, including pictures.' He describes himself as obsessed with news, and makes a living by training journalists, speaking and other ancillary work to support the website. The site brings him a profile which brings in the other work. Like major news organisations in the past, his solo international reporting is subsidised by other activities.

> *I took some photographs at a football match and put together a slide show for the site. I've never thought of myself as a photographer. But from that I was asked to write a piece for Focus on Africa, I got a speaking engagement and asked to present a seminar at the BBC. I was also asked to mount a photographic exhibition. I made more than I would from a straightforward commission.*

He sees his role as a journalistic bridge. 'If you can go somewhere very odd and interpret it with your own culture and values, it brings that world into other people's living rooms and has value.'[54] His site has become a must-visit source for news agencies and other correspondents interested in Rwanda.

Deborah Bonello set up Mexicoreporter.com in 2007 as a site for digital reporting about Mexico and in particular video-journalism. 'I didn't want to do it in the old way because I could see that was on the way out. I wanted to do something innovative, do something that would get media attention.' Much of her work was investigative or feature-led; original entrepreneurial journalism rather than breaking news which she left to the news agencies. Crucially she set out to offer specialist journalism which could put events in Mexico into an informed context. The site acted as a shop window for her work and helped her get commissions from the *LA Times*, the *Guardian*, the *Independent* and finally a job at the *FT*.

> *No-one else was doing what I was doing. The benefit of the site was that they could see what I was doing consistently. And the work I did for the LA Times and the Guardian gave me a standard of trust which brought in other work and supported the site.*

---

[54] Interview with author, March 2010.

Freelance journalists have always made an important contribution to international news and the opportunities to do so are now greater than ever thanks to low-cost digital technology. As Marcus Brauchli from the *Washington Post* points out, we may be entering a new golden age:

> *There are more reporters around the world writing for*
> *an international audience than there have ever been. The*
> *quality and depth of coverage are greater than they have ever*
> *been. There is a great deal of nostalgia for the newspaper*
> *correspondent of yore, but when the Baltimore Sun had a*
> *single correspondent in Asia and he got to go to Korea or the*
> *Philippines for a week having never been before, was he really*
> *bringing greater authority and knowledge to his readers?*
> *If he was your single source of information about Asia you*
> *probably got a pretty skewed version of reality.[55]*

What he may have uniquely offered, of course, was an understanding of the Baltimore readership and how to interest them in Asian affairs. One of the core roles of a foreign correspondent is to act as a bridge between the living rooms at home and an alien place on the other side of the world. Technology however, has brought the world closer to our living rooms in new and vivid ways.

Staff correspondents now can have blogs as well as their regular reporting outlets. This allows for a more informal, and sometimes insightful, perspective on their work which in turn may appeal to a wider audience. When the UK's *Channel 4 News* correspondent, Jonathan Rugman, reported from the Haiti earthquake he reflected on his experience in a blog on his return.

> *Journalists can be caught unawares, their professionalism*
> *quite possibly enhanced by explosions of sheer empathy. Jon*
> *Snow cried after one interview in Haiti. I cried last year after*
> *making a film about the sexual abuse of children in Kenya,*
> *so clearly this hack can crack in some circumstances and*
> *without empathy, how are you going to make your viewers*
> *care, which they must if they are to donate money, which*
> *of course makes our jobs that much more worthwhile? And*
> *without empathy, how are you going to rise to the verbal*
> *challenge of matching the harrowing pictures your terrific*
> *cameraman has shot?[56]*

---

[55] Interview with author, Feb. 2010.
[56] http://blogs.channel4.com/snowblog/2010/02/02/shaken-but-not-stirred-confessions-of-a-haiti-reporter/.

It is unlikely he would have broadcast anything of that kind, but the comments on his post make it clear the readers appreciated a candid reflection. It provided a more profound understanding of, and empathy with, the story.

Online journalism can be more personal and less distant – which has a significant impact on the style of reporting. The informality of blogs allows reporters to reveal more of themselves as individuals and personalities. There are editorial risks around this of course – but also significant advantages in appealing to new and younger readers and allowing readers to identify with the writer by bringing greater vividness to their reporting. Blogs can also offer a depth of specialism which general news services struggle to provide, allowing opportunities for freelances and others to provide journalism which is differentiated from the mainstream coverage of major news organisations.

The internet is a global distribution system and provides the opportunity for those who wish to find out about the world to be better informed than ever before. Newsdesks and reporters can be better informed too. A point again picked up by Marcus Brauchli: 'If you want the authentic version of events in Pakistan, say, you can read Dawn.com to find out what's happening.'[57]

Or as Ethan Zuckerman explains:

> *A reader interested in news from Ghana doesn't have to rely*
> *on her local newspaper, or even the New York Times, to cover*
> *Ghanaian news – she can access the websites of half a dozen*
> *Ghanaian newspapers, the online presence of radio stations*
> *like Joy.FM, and dedicated internet news sites like Ghanaweb.*
> *Via web streaming, several Ghanaian television stations*
> *can be viewed over the internet, including the Ghanaian*
> *Broadcasting Corporation.*[58]

This growth in digital opportunities to consume is in contrast to the chill across professional newsgathering discussed earlier. News distribution channels have expanded but professional, integrated newsgathering has shrunk and risks being overwhelmed by new demands.

Digital newsgathering may be cheaper, but the additional productivity is soaked up by the expansion in channels and outlets, all reflecting a similar core agenda. An exponential growth in output rests on a reduced base of professional international newsgathering. In such circumstances it is hardly surprising that opinion-led journalism is drowning out fact or evidence-based journalism.

The supply of conventional news is now substantially dwarfed by the

---

[57] Interview with author, Feb. 2010.
[58] Zuckerman, 'International News', in *Media Re:Public* (Berkman Center, Havard, 2008).

number of sites offering information. In 2006, Dr Chris Paterson at Leeds University analysed the content of popular news websites. He found that 50 per cent of the content of major news sites was supplied by the news agencies, principally Reuters and the AP (for ABC News the figure was 91 per cent, for the BBC 9 per cent). Looking at news portals run by internet companies the figure was even higher – 85 per cent. This raises the spectre of more and more sites with less and less on them.

Paterson concluded:

> *The evolution of the online news agency has laid bare the news industries' near total dependence on a few wholesale news providers and the limitations on public discourse that it inevitably yields. … While the online news industry continues to pretend for the moment that it brings readers a diversity of reporting on world news, it is a pretence which cannot last. … in the longer term the industry must invest in more original reporting as an alternative to the few genuinely international news organisations now on offer, and give more prominence to buying, and properly translating, original non-English language reporting from around the world. Without such change, new media will continue to present to most users the dangerous illusion of multiple perspectives which actually emanate from very few sources.*[59]

Similarly, the Project for Excellence in Journalism in the US found in its 2006 report on American journalism that Google News, increasingly a mainstream portal for news, did not live up to its promise of news diversity either. An analysis of one day's coverage of Google News found it offered some 14,000 stories on its front page, but they were actually accounts of the same 24 stories from different news sources – and many of those provided by the news agencies.[60]

Regular consumers of news are often struck by the similarity of content across different organisations. There seems to be a core agenda or set of issues which all organisations report simultaneously. It is unlikely these are the only important or interesting things happening in the world at that time. Rather, it is a consequence of the herd instinct of news organisations – feeling they cannot risk not reporting something a competitor reports: resource limitations and a cultural consensus in news judgement. In 1996 Stephen Hess analysed the news output of the US TV networks and came to this conclusion:

---

[59] Chris Paterson, 'News Agency Dominance in International News on the Internet', Centre for International Communications Research, Leeds University, May 2006.
[60] PEJ 'State of the News Media', 2006 (www.stateofthemedia.org).

This sameness should not come as a surprise. The three networks have similar resources and the same constraints of time, money and personnel. Their correspondents, producers and crews are drawn from the same pool of talent. Indeed, in some cases they are the same people.

Although technology and the internet provide huge opportunities to increase the supply of international news and the diversity of reporting, most mainstream news sites have concentrated on building their voice and reach in the market rather than building their range or depth of content. Although organisations like ABC News, CNN, the BBC and some newspapers are investing in lightweight digital newsgathering teams, the agenda they report remains constrained by cultural, financial and competitive pressures.

The vast increase in channels of news and information has soaked up the increased productivity in professional newsgathering enabled by digital technology. Consequently, the supply of international news from professional organisations has shrunk as demand has increased with the proliferation of new services.

However, other players beyond journalism are stepping up to tell their own stories. The internet has allowed open access to the public space where once the media played the role of gatekeeper. Any stakeholder in an international event or issue can now communicate directly with the public they seek to influence rather than have to rely on the judgements of journalists to mediate their story. Those who were once reported upon can now report themselves.

So when in 2008 the Israeli Defence Force sent aircraft to attack Hamas militants in Gaza, they also opened up a front in the media, launching their own YouTube channel, a blog for IDF spokesmen, and the Israeli Consulate in New York held a news conference on Twitter. Israeli soldiers were allowed to update reports on the unfolding war. Their aim was to 'make information easily available to those who are interested'.

The *Haaretz* newspaper quoted IDF spokeswoman Major Avital Leibovich saying: 'The blogosphere and the new media are basically a war zone in a battle for world opinion.' She added that the YouTube channel is an important part of Israel's attempt to explain its actions abroad. 'In modern-day warfare, some battles are conducted through the media', said Gideon Doron, former chairman of the government agency that oversaw the privatisation of television and radio services in Israel. 'Many of the victories of modern warfare are mediated by the media,' Doron said. 'We have Internet and all kinds of modern communication, and the Israeli military apparently decided that it has to broadcast its message through these tools.'[61]

---

[61] Haaretz.com, 20 July 2010.

The initiative has predictably provoked criticism among blogs and pro-Arab websites and been dismissed as propaganda. Equally, Palestinian supporters are just as active on Twitter and other social media. However, the key point is that anyone with an interest in the event can hear direct from the protagonist rather than via an edited version from a newspaper or broadcaster.

Another, less controversial, example of a government seeking direct communication with the public via the internet is the website set up by the British Foreign and Commonwealth Office for the G20 meeting in London in April 2009. The FCO's then Director of Strategy, Ian Hargreaves, explained that in advance of the summit they decided that 'government to government' diplomacy was decreasing in the light of wider public engagement and for the G20 summit they should seek to host as open a dialogue and facilitate as much access as they could.[62]

They built a website offering information in 40 languages but also decided to make it a digital hub to aggregate content and discussion about the summit's themes.[63] In this way it was a channel for government information and views, but also an open debating channel. They partnered with networks and blog groups and NGOs around the world to try to hold the widest discussion possible. To their surprise, the biggest audience was in South Korea, because they had a strong partner and there are high levels of online participation there. It included an Academics forum, a youth debate, blog aggregation and socialising the content through sites like Digg, Facebook and Twitter.

Clearly experimental, it not only took the opportunity to take the British government's view direct to the public, but also sought to play a wider role in aggregating all other content and discussion – a role normally left to the news media. Again for anyone around the world interested in the summit or its themes it was an essential source of information, quite separate from any independent news operation.

It is not only governments that take advantage of these opportunities. As BP struggled to control the Deepwater Horizon oil spill in the Gulf of Mexico in 2010 they were subject to hostile political comment and media coverage. Although BP already had a website which featured their operations, they expanded this with significant reporting of their own about their emergency operations and crisis management.[64] It included regular technical updates, behind the scenes coverage of the control centre, video feeds of the spill and the rescue operations, blogs from BP employees, reporting of the compensation process and aggregation of other coverage. In response of course, there were many other websites highly critical of BP's crisis handling. Greenpeace for example offered extensive negative comment and analysis on BP's activities

---

[62] Speech to Ax:ess 'Future of news' conference, London, July 2010.
[63] www.londonsummit.gov.uk/en/.
[64] www.bp.com/extendedsectiongenericarticle.do?categoryId=40&contentId=7061813.

and strategy. For anyone interested in the issue, both sites would provide more information, depth and analysis, albeit from different perspectives, than could be contained in a single news report.

It is arguable, in the face of relentless criticism from politicians and the media, whether BP's reporting of itself held much credibility or made a difference to wider news coverage. However it was at least one guaranteed avenue through which BP could tell the story as they saw it, unmediated. Other commercial companies are increasingly taking the opportunity to tell their own stories – from their CSR or Fair Trade initiatives to showcasing brands and products – in the hope of building consumer loyalty. They all contribute to the new flows of information in a global digital environment.

Financial institutions essentially operate their own private news networks, with country and industry analysts providing insight beyond the news for staff and clients. Such private flows of information are what provide major City firms with their competitive edge.

NGOs from Oxfam to Amnesty to Open Society now directly contribute to public debate in their areas of concern. If your particular interest is Kazakhstan, then the Soros Foundation-funded website,[65] launched to promote democracy and civil society development there, will be of more use to you than the foreign pages of most daily newspapers. As Glenda Cooper has discovered, charities are increasingly taking on the role of newsgathering themselves – taking pictures and filing copy direct to news desks.

> *The two agencies who led this charge in the U.K. were Oxfam and Christian Aid. They both hired former journalists to run their press operations as pseudo-newsrooms. Both agencies pushed the idea of press officers as 'fireman' reporters — on the ground as soon as possible after a disaster occurred to gather and film information themselves. Oxfam protocol written for their UK press office in 2007, for example, demanded that a press officer sent to a disaster should use an international cellphone, a local cellphone, a satellite phone, a laptop (capable of transmitting stills and short video clips), and a digital camera.[66]*

She points out that journalism and NGOs have always had a symbiotic relationship, exchanging access and information for publicity. But in this blurring of the boundaries, the NGOs need to be clear whether they are acting as reporters or advocates. And if news organisations use NGO material

---

[65] www.soros.kz/en.html.
[66] 'NGOs and the News', Nieman Journalism Lab, Dec. 2009: www.niemanlab.org/2009/12/glenda-cooper-when-lines-between-ngo-and-news-organization-blur/

it must be transparently flagged as such.

There are risks and opportunities in this opening of the public realm. While it is healthy for any organisation or individual to tell its own story – and any of them is entitled to put forward their best case – the lack of independent scrutiny risks a corruption of public debate. As Paul Starr points out, journalism for hire is not necessarily in the public interest:

> *Online there are few clear markers to distinguish blogs and other sites that are being financed to promote a viewpoint from news sites operated independently on the basis of professional rules of reporting. So the danger is not just more corruption of government and business – it is more corruption of journalism itself.*[67]

The evangelists of course hope that such sites are self-regulating, with the scrutiny of bloggers and others highlighting errors, distortions, omissions and deceit. But there's no guarantee or accountability surrounding that.

The current dynamic, where professional newsgathering is shrinking as other actors storm through the gate to express themselves directly to the public, raises questions about the ability of journalism to fulfil its public function of investigation and verification of information. Shrinking newsrooms risk being overwhelmed by the scale of information now available and may lack the skills to check, verify and analyse it all.

Eyewitness reporting

To properly understand the complexity of events – particularly in a crisis or war zone – takes skill, time and experience, all of which are disappearing from the world of foreign reporting. Mark Danner, who writes for the *New York Review of Books*, and is Professor of Journalism at Berkeley Journalism School, talks about the process of understanding deeply complex events:

> *From far away such stories come to us with an order readily imposed, often a moral or ideological one: good versus bad, developed versus underdeveloped, us versus them. The closer one gets, the less certain things become … After a few weeks or days of looking and listening and learning, you realise that despite all the work, you know nothing. Then truth dawns: it is because of all the work that you know nothing. You have stripped away the borrowed preconceptions and secondhand conclusions and attained a cherished state. From here you*

---

[67] Paul Starr, 'Goodbye to the Age of Newspapers', *New Republic*, March 2009.

might begin to understand for yourself.[68]

The importance of an experienced professional journalist witnessing events with time to consider them is little discussed and easily glossed over in discussions of the new opportunities of 'digital reporting'. But as Bill Schiller of the *Toronto Star* put it:

> *If we hope to explain what Lyndon Johnson's late presidential adviser Jack Valenti once called a foreign culture's 'ancestral rhythms' we have to go to where those rhythms play out – and watch as they are rearranged on a daily basis. We've got to get close enough to listen – and understand what we are hearing.*[69]

Or, as he quotes UPI's Leon Daniel once saying, 'if it isn't based on shoe-leather reporting isn't worth a bucket of beans'.

Philip Gourevitch has reported regularly from Rwanda since the genocide in the mid-1990s. He describes the importance of eyewitness reporting in physical terms:

> *Being there brings everything to one's work that one can't achieve at a distance – you have to see a place, walk around in it, touch it, smell it, feel its changes directly, you have to go into people's homes to understand them ... you cannot seriously report on life without going to where it is lived. You can insert yourself into the meta-story, as bloggers and political commentators do, on diplomatic, legal, international matters, But it's really simple – if you're not there you're not reporting a place, you're reporting about the way some people who may or may not be there are talking about a place.*[70]

There are no substitutes for a prolonged process of firsthand engagement to understand and report what is being witnessed. This may be the most valuable element of foreign reporting at risk from the changes underway.

Harriet Sherwood was previously Foreign Editor at the *Guardian* and is now their Jerusalem correspondent.

> *The wire services ... provide comprehensive, rapidly updated and usually accurate coverage of the main news events on*

---

[68] M. Danner, *Stripping Bare the Body* (2009).

[69] B. Schiller, 'Even in Digital Age, "Being There" Still Matters in Foreign Reporting', *Nieman Reports*, Sept. 2010.

[70] Interview with author, Sept. 2010.

> *a given day. So a correspondent's role is surely to go beyond that, to dig out the stories that aren't immediate 'news', to provide context and analysis, to allow those whose voices are routinely drowned out by the big 'players' to be heard. But that requires an investment of time (and often money) which inevitably has become harder with the instant and constant demands of digital journalism.[71]*

Instead, resources are being withdrawn and journalists and newsrooms are ever more reliant on the internet – particularly the tsunami of social media.

Correspondents in future will find a core function being the verification, assessment and analysis of information others have published without the time and resources to report and 'unlearn' their preconceptions, as Danner puts it.

Social media

In 2009, 500 billion minutes per month were spent on Facebook globally, there were an average of 55 million messages per day on Twitter, YouTube served 2 billion video streams per day. The average American user spent six and a half hours per month on Facebook, used Google for an average of two hours per month but only spent about half an hour on CNN – slightly more than the average news website. Traditional media are lagging behind in online popularity.[72]

Social media are a global phenomenon but local in character. In the USA and Europe Facebook may dominate, but in South America it is more likely to be Orkut people turn to; in Russia, LiveJournal or Kontakte, in China RenRen or the search engine Baidu, in Korea Cyworld or for the Japanese Mixi and so on.

Social media are a source of information for journalists, but also provide real competition to traditional news organisations. According to the Pew 'Internet and American Life' Project, social media are significantly more popular than traditional news sites for internet users in the USA. They estimate that:

- 61 per cent of Americans get their news online as against 17 per cent from newspaper;

- 51 per cent of social networking users in the US get news from people they follow;

---

[71] 'From Our Own Correspondent', *Guardian*, 27 Sept. 2010.
[72] Nielsen internet ratings. http://en-us.nielsen.com/content/nielsen/en_us/product_families/nielsen_buzzmetrics.html.

- 46 per cent of Americans get their news from between four and six online media platforms each day;

- 37 per cent of US internet users say they create or react to news.[73]

These sites are the new online cities and neighbourhood bars, places where people gather to mix, chat and exchange views. As such, like real cities and bars, they provide the raw material of journalism. Correspondents' jobs will increasingly involve taking what they hear online and applying professional journalistic practices to verify and contextualise it. But they are also disintermediating news services by becoming the 'turn to' sites when news happens.

The success of social media in alerting people to breaking news has raised the question of its effectiveness as a 'free news agency'. From the Asian tsunami in 2004 to the Mumbai terrorist attacks, Iranian protests, to the Haiti earthquake in 2010 social media have worked as an early alert. Traditional news operations are embracing social media as a consequence – using them to alert their audiences to breaking news. As Matthew Weaver, a blogger at the *Guardian*, puts it, when rallies and conflicts occur, 'first the tweets come, then the pictures, then the video and then the wires'.[74]

Jon Williams, the BBC's World News Editor says, 'What I principally want from the news agencies is a tip off service. If Social Media can play that role it calls into question the value of expensive agency contracts.'[75] The BBC has a 'UGC Hub' staffed 24 hours a day by up to eight journalists, to handle material sent in by the public and to act as an interface between social media and the BBC's programmes. Their Director of Global News, Peter Horrocks, recently told staff that using social media was now essential to their work. The BBC World Service uses it not only for breaking news of major events but also original newsgathering, as Peter Horrocks explained:

> *Classic examples are situations where it is hard to report from. In northern Nigeria, for example, we are using mobile phones which we provided to villages. In each village there is one person who is known as 'the keeper of the mobile'. This was a way we learnt about a government confrontation with a village about land rights.[76]*

---

[73] www.pewinternet.org.
[74] N. Newman, *The Rise of Social Media and its Impact on Mainstream Journalism* (RISJ 2009).
[75] Interview with author, May 2010.
[76] www.guardian.co.uk/media/pda/2010/feb/10/peter-horrocks-social-media.

If Twitter is serving breaking-news needs, internet search sites can feed the appetite for depth and analysis, as Rebecca MacKinnon, a former CNN journalist and academic, points out:

> *When people go to Google looking for something, they end up on blogs, on research reports, on press releases, on think tank sites – whatever organisations are most skilled at putting information out on the web and optimising it for search. In Mainstream Media you only learn what the newsdesk thinks you should know … If you want quantity of information on any subject it's there, but you have to take the initiative. In the old days there was no way you could find out about it.[77]*

Under these circumstances, mainstream news may prove to be the least well informed source for specialist subjects and analysis of international affairs unless it too uses the resources available, employing professional information skills to better inform the general audience.

The question is whether the internet can live up to this potential for informing people about the world. Evidence suggests that very few, outside information professionals, take the trouble to search in depth for international news. Ninety-five per cent of online news readership is on domestic news sites.[78] In addition, most people in the world, particularly in developing countries, don't have internet access. And according to the OpenNet Initiative, more states are attempting to control what content their citizens can see.[79]

Most countries are net importers of internet content rather than exporters – the internet is dominated by content from the USA and, increasingly, China (Mandarin is now the most used language on the internet globally).

There is a risk of what Ethan Zuckerman has called 'imaginary cosmopolitanism' where we believe we have a global perspective, but forget most of our consumption is local. Guy Berger, Professor of Journalism at Rhodes University, recognises that only a minority of users seek out information from around the world and that much of what the internet provides in online news is national or local, but he remains optimistic that it can provide richer, global, pan-national coverage.

> *The internet could enable every user to experience the extent and excitement of knowledge of a wider world that is ever more integrated and one in which, digital divides notwithstanding, news content about and by developing*

---

[77] Interview with author, Feb. 2010.
[78] Google Ad Planner 6/2010: www.ted.com/talks/ethan_zuckerman.html.
[79] www.access-controlled.net/.

*countries can increasingly be contributed. While there are
indeed centrifugal tendencies pushing some First World
internet news content towards hyperlocal myopia, there
are also countervailing dynamics that in the long run give
impetus to a hyperglobal dimension.*[80]

This provides the opportunity for a greater diversity of voices and opinions
to be aired in reporting any particular issue – and a greater range of potential
sources for establishing what has happened.

As Kathleen Carroll, Executive Editor of the Associated Press puts it:

*There may be fewer bureaux but there are new tools and
more news sites. We may be seeing a new blossoming of
international correspondence – from unexpected directions.
Other agencies and partnerships will blossom, a wider
audience will be brought to local journalists, there may be
new alliances that will bring news from places where it's
difficult to report.*[81]

She refers to the flowering of new online sites and resources which are
reporting the world from outside the framework of traditional news. Here are
just some examples.

• When a major earthquake hit Haiti in January 2010, some
of the first reports and pictures from those caught up in
the disaster came through Twitter. Online monitoring
service Nielsen reported Twitter was the main source of
discussion and information about the crisis: 'While most
online consumers rely on traditional media for coverage
of the quake, they are turning to Twitter and blogs to share
information, react to the situation and rally support.'[82]

• The blog aggregator Global Voices, surfaces opinion
and reporting in blogs around the world, in a range of
translated languages, that for most people would otherwise
go unnoticed. The front page, on one day (20 July 2010),
comprised contributions from India, Thailand, Ecuador,
Brazil, Ivory Coast, Jamaica, Puerto Rico, Israel, Colombia,

[80] Guy Berger, 'How the Internet Impacts on International News', *International Communication Gazette*, 2009.
[81] Interview with author, March 2010.
[82] http://blog.nielsen.com/nielsenwire/online_mobile/social-media-and-mobile-texting-a-major-source-of-info-and-aid-for-earthquake-in-haiti/

Palestine, Jordan, Zambia, Lebanon, Slovakia and Paraguay, with hundreds of countries represented deeper in the site. They, like all blogs, reflect personal experience, opinion and occasionally revelation.[83]

- Wikileaks is perhaps the best example of online investigative resources. It is a controversial, volunteer-driven website that publishes and comments on leaked documents alleging government and corporate misconduct, for example, their publication of 90,000 US military records from the war in Afghanistan – the biggest leak of military documents since the Pentagon Papers in 1971.[84] The documents were given to three newspapers in advance to allow them to examine in detail and publish simultaneously. Subsequently the organisation was criticised by the military and news organisations for failing to redact the names of Afghan sources.[85] There are other examples, like the longer established Center for Investigative Reporting.[86]

- Mapping services like Ushahidi[87] are providing insight into disaster relief and reporting. Growing out of the disturbances following the 2007 elections in Kenya, the service collates reports sent in via SMS, email, Twitter and the web to provide a map of incidents around any major event. It supported emergency relief in Haiti, receiving 100,000 reports in four days. It has now been used in Chile, Pakistan, Congo, Peru, China and more. Al Jazeera used the platform to allow Israelis and Palestinians to update reports of attacks during the 2008 Gaza conflict. The following year it was used to monitor the Indian elections.

- The aggregation of data is increasingly making maps and analysis easily available online. Silobreaker.com is an automated aggregator which also makes links between search terms and offers the results in graphic as well as text form – providing context which might otherwise be missed.

---

[83] www.globalvoicesonline.org.
[84] www.wikileaks.org.
[85] www.guardian.co.uk/world/blog/2010/jul/26/afghanistan-war-logs-wikileaks.
[86] www.centerforinvestigativereporting.org/.
[87] www.ushahidi.com.

These are essentially 'non-professional' information services enabled by technology which contribute to international news flows and to public debate. The contribution of individuals and sites outside of professional journalism is becoming increasingly important – and not just for the typical eyewitness 'citizen journalist' pictures or accounts.

In his book, *Supermedia*, Charlie Beckett suggests 'Networked Journalism' – where the public help inform and direct professional journalists – is a way for journalism to meet the challenges of the digital era. He believes it can restore trust in journalism, help tell stories with greater accuracy and context, connect different people in different places, put humanity at the heart of journalism and therefore retain the audience's attention.

He quotes the description by the Annenberg Center for Communications of new information flows in the digital age:

> *With the advent of the multimedia internet, publics can traffic in both professional and personal media in new forms of many-to-many communication that often route around commercial media distribution. Personal media and communications technologies such as telephony, email, text messaging and everyday photography and journaling are colliding with commercial and mass media such as television, film and commercial music.*[88]

This is not the place for a detailed analysis of networked journalism, except to note how technology is enabling the public to contribute to, partake in and consume international news and information in deeper ways than ever before.

As well as 'non-professional' services there are of course innovative new sites which aim to deliver news to professional standards. The internet has provided opportunities for a fresh approach to professional and commercial news production – although innovation largely rests outside established media.

Examples

Global Post[89] was launched in 2009 as a foreign news service on the internet with the mission to 'redefine international news for the digital age'. The CEO Philip Balboni, a former cable news executive, says:

> *There is a substantial audience for thoughtful international reporting but for mass media people whose whole predicate*

---

[88] Annenberg Center for Communications, *Networked Publics*, USC, 2006.
[89] www.globalpost.com/.

*is to reach the largest audience it's not a priority for them.
We had half a dozen core constituencies in mind for the
content we helped create from the heavy news consumer to
the globally oriented business person to college and university
students.*

The site is not yet profitable but is on track with its business plan, he says. It is an internet news site with reports from freelance correspondents who are paid small retainers. However the model is now extending to news syndication, with CBS news among their corporate customers. Balboni believes there has to be more innovation in journalism and in advertising.

*The innovation in journalism is pathetic. Journalism needs
a sense of adventure and entrepreneurship and then it can
create something good and sustainable. At the moment online
advertising cannot support by itself the kind of journalism we
want to see.*[90]

Ground Report[91] is a citizen journalist portal which allows anyone to contribute material for international consumption. It focuses on original material only. CEO Rachel Sterne says she created it in response to the lack of international news in the West. 'I thought there must be a better way for people to share stories, create emotional engagements about the world.' It is funded by a mixture of advertising and foundation support.[92] During the Mumbai terrorist attacks in 2008 it beat mainstream news organisations to breaking news and offered perspectives only locals witnessing events could provide.

Tehran Bureau is an online news magazine covering politics, foreign affairs, culture and society in Iran and the Iranian diaspora. Its mission statement states:

*Tehran Bureau is a virtual bureau connecting journalists,
Iran experts and readers all over the world. It was launched
in 2009 as a virtual news bureau, with regular contributors
and professional journalists specialising in Iranian affairs.
It is now part funded by the PBS TV series 'Frontline' which
hosts its Web site and provides editorial support.*[93]

---

[90] Interview with author, March 2010.
[91] www.groundreport.com/.
[92] http://images.businessweek.com/ss/09/04/0403_social_entrepreneurs/27.htm.
[93] www.pbs.org/wgbh/pages/frontline/tehranbureau/.

Demotix is a photo-journalism agency which started as a citizen journalism platform but swiftly evolved to a professional model. Founder Turi Munthe launched it in 2009 – today it handles about 20,000 images and videos a month. He says:

> *News has shrunk – there's a growing sense that all the sources are the same, a massive reliance on AP and Reuters globally across every media. The idea was to build a network which harvested original reporting around the world untied to the agencies and do it on a variable cost base.*

He says he doesn't believe citizen journalism really exists – 'you have witnesses with the means to communicate, it's not journalism'. A lot of effort is put into the verification of images submitted in order to support high editorial standards and build reputation. During the Iran protests in 2009 Demotix supplied two front-page pictures for the *New York Times* in four days. Munthe sees the site as a community of professional photo-journalists. They are now syndicating material, taking advertising and entering into distribution partnerships – expecting to be profitable by 2012.[94]

Publish 2[95] is an online news exchange which hopes to change news distribution models by supporting greater partnership between news organisations. Founder Scott Karp describes it as the eBay of news – enabling the simple exchange of content and taking a transaction fee for providing the opportunity. 'The old mode was where each news organisation operated in a silo unto itself. That's how the technology worked. Now we have to organise a more networked, collaborative model with the economics intertwined.'

None of these are yet profitable in their own right – and they have many predecessors which have failed. However they represent strong examples of online experimentation around news. It is notable that most of this innovation comes from new start-ups rather from within established media organisations. They have no legacy costs to cover and no ingrained established model of news production to transition away from. So rather than bear staff costs or the fixed costs of bureaux, for example, Ground Report or Demotix support the work of freelance journalists who happen to be where news has happened. Separate business models for news production and news distribution are being found, rather than seeing them as necessarily integrated. As a consequence, new forms of partnership, collaboration and syndication are emerging.

---

[94] www.demotix.com interview with author, June 2010.
[95] www.publish2.com/.

Conclusion

- Digital technology has cut the costs of international newsgathering and the barriers to entry for new services and platforms.

- As a result there are more sources of news than ever before, some professional news sources, many others from freelances, governments, NGOs, companies, blogs and social media.

- These new players are both sources for professional journalists, but also competing for public attention.

- Much of the increased productivity for professional newsgathering has been soaked up by the exponential rise in new platforms and services.

- This has meant a shrinking of original professional journalism with greater dependence on the news agencies.

- Also at risk in the face of an exponential increase in information is the ability of journalists to verify and mediate material produced by those with an interest in the issue reported.

- The core responsibility of journalists to bear witness to events is also under pressure.

- There is significant innovation underway – but much of it unproven in business terms and most of it from outside established media.

- There is a new emphasis on collaboration and partnership between professional journalism, non-journalism organisations and the public.

4. Globalisation

The growing interconnectedness of the world, through global communications, ease of travel, increasing migration and more, is changing expectations of international reporting. What was once 'foreign' is now better known. For diaspora communities, news from overseas can be news from home. In increasingly multicultural societies, national identity is more complex and a white middle-class male reporter may not be an adequate cultural bridge between the country he is reporting and the audience at home. The importance of diversity is as true in international reporting as any other area of life.

In 2008, the Managing Editor of Global Voices, Solana Larsen, made this provocative statement to the Media Re:Public conference in the USA:

> *How many more years will we have to watch foreign correspondents parachute into a region and pretend they know what's going on? How many more reports coming out of the Middle East from hotel rooftops will be delivered by people who do not speak Arabic or know what the Green Zone in Iraq was called before coalition forces arrived? Sooner or later qualified local perspectives will become what people prefer to hear rather than what editors defer to when a situation becomes too dangerous for Western journalists to report from. It's wrong not to have news from a faraway place simply because there is no longer money to fly foreign correspondents there.[96]*

It is a view others endorse. Bill Thompson, broadcaster and digital consultant, agrees:

> *The idea of the Foreign Correspondent is a relic of a pre-*

---

[96] Speech at Media Re:Public, Berkman Center conference, Annenberg Center Los Angeles, March 2008.

*networked age. As the internet spreads there are more and
more places where we can simply ask those who are living
through events what they think of them and seek insights
and analysis from those who know the people and the places
involved. This change will ripple through the newsgathering
departments of every major media organisation.[97]*

Such a view of course favours sites like Global Voices and the inclinations
of digital evangelists. By painting Western correspondents as underinformed
and transitory it overlooks genuine journalistic or specialist expertise, talent
to communicate and bridge cultures, and deep experience, which many of
them possess.

However it is also true that an unspoken secret of foreign news for many
years was that journalists could 'get away' with more because their subjects
would never read, see or hear what had been said. That is no longer true.
Globalisation has forced greater levels of transparency around international
news – with a consequent pressure to deliver greater accuracy, fairness and
accountability. If your interviewees and subjects know what you are saying
about them, you need to get it right.

Diversity and local staff

There is no doubt that news organisations are thinking harder about local staff,
diversity and the benefits they can bring. Sean Maguire, Reuters' Editor of
Political and General News, sees significant changes to his agency's staffing mix:

> *We employ a lot fewer Brits than we used to as we shift
> further away from the old colonial/commonwealth model of
> white males spending a career moving from assignment to
> assignment. Staff is much more likely to be female, younger
> and nationals of the country they work in. Apart from cost,
> issues of equity and fairness in employment are driving that
> shift. Additionally news consumers … demand higher levels
> of instant expertise in reporting – to deliver that you need
> correspondents who speak a local language, are immersed in
> local political and economic life and have contacts developed
> over years.[98]*

His Editor-in-Chief, David Schlesinger, says Reuters employs journalists from
90 different countries:

---

[97] www.fromthefrontline.co.uk: 'The Rise and Demise of the Foreign Correspondent'.
[98] Interview with author, March 2010.

*Local journalists are vital to getting the story right. They
know their areas; they have the expertise and the contacts.
Many come from the best local media, so they have years
of experience covering the story and the key players. Many
want to stay in their home countries and make a career in the
place they know best. Others want to join the international
ranks ... this pattern is as true for an American who joins
an agency in New York as for an Indian who joins in New
Delhi.*[99]

His competitors at the AP are moving in the same direction. Kathleen Carroll,
their Executive Editor, says the agency has worked hard to move from a
traditional model of ex-pat correspondents to a more equal partnership with
local staff. 'It's not just economic, it simply wasn't healthy. It's more effective
to have local newsgatherers. We can form new career paths so we don't have
stagnant careers for locals and travelling ex-pats.' However she believes a
mix of local staff and ex-pats works best. 'It's good to have them cover their
country alongside someone who is an outsider. It provides coverage that is
authoritative but also open to the curiosity that a non-local may have.'[100]

News agencies, serving global audiences, may be exceptions. They have to
operate in the widest range of countries and their journalism cannot reflect
national points of view or biases. They have a long history of employing
local staff, often reporting in their own languages. But now some major
broadcasters and newspapers – particularly those with global audiences – are
also following suit.

Jon Williams, the BBC's World News Editor, believes attitudes towards local
correspondents are changing rapidly.

*Take Sanjoy Majumder for example. He was taken on as
an online reporter in our Delhi bureau but brought into the
mainstream of our coverage three years ago. Now he packages
for the (flagship bulletin) Ten O'Clock News and appears on
Radio 4. Eighteen months ago they would not have used him.
UK programmes often want someone who understands the
UK audience and can explain a story to them in their own
terms. But often that's not the case.*

He explains why he appointed Kim Ghattas, a Lebanese correspondent, to
report the State Department in Washington. 'I wanted someone who's been

---

[99] Schlesinger, 'The Future of News Services', in Owen and Purdey (eds), *International News Reporting* (2009).
[100] Interview with author, Feb. 2010.

on the receiving end of US policy. Her presence in Washington marks us out. She can unlock access – Hillary Clinton seeks her out and is interested in what she's got to say.'

In planning how the BBC should cover the death of Nelson Mandela he recognised it would be unacceptable to report such an event with only white people. So he has appointed Milton Nkosi, a former producer and bureau chief, as correspondent and part of the commentary team. 'He can offer the authentic voice of black South Africa and also unlock access for us.'[101]

The BBC World Service has also begun to see how many of the regular contributors to its 32 language services can report in English – seeking to unlock local expertise for a wider global audience. The BBC's James Miles recalls the success of two local colleagues during the Israeli attacks on Gaza in 2008:

> *Local reporters as foreign correspondents are often*
> *spectacularly successful. In Gaza, Rushdi Abu Alouf and*
> *Hamada Abu Qammar worked behind the scenes for the BBC*
> *as a producer and organiser helping incoming teams arrange*
> *interviews. In December 2008, Israel carried out an offensive*
> *into Gaza to stop Palestinian rocket fire, and its government*
> *closed the border so that most foreign correspondents were*
> *unable to get into Gaza. Rushdi and Hamada were there so*
> *they filed the reports that correspondents would normally*
> *file. For the next few weeks they provided clear, lucid and fair*
> *minded coverage of Israel's offensive in Gaza. They helped*
> *me see the role of a foreign correspondent in a different way.*
> *… I welcome them as colleagues who will give us a fresh*
> *perspective on the news from their countries … Now many*
> *see the advent of local reporters as a welcome step towards a*
> *post-colonial reporting world.[102]*

For Al Jazeera, diversity in recruitment was essential from the outset. Ibrahim Helal, a senior executive, explains:

> *Al Jazeera usually recruits correspondents from WITHIN the*
> *country, so we usually do not have the ex-pat correspondent*
> *problems. And because Al Jazeera (Arabic or English) recruit*
> *from a global market, we have been enjoying the benefit of*
> *having multi-national newsrooms. At any given moment you*

---

[101] Interview with author May 2010.
[102] J. Miles, 'Correspondents: They Come in Different Shapes and Sizes', *Nieman Reports*, Sept. 2010.

*may find more than 10 nationalities in the newsroom and
more in the building.*

This policy stretches to correspondents and teams in the field as well: 'This has
always been an essential part of what Al Jazeera calls "Journalism of Depth" as
opposed to "parachuting journalism" which is adopted by many international
media.'[103]

There is a strong sense from international news organisations that they
not only have the opportunity but the responsibility to train and employ
more local journalists to report directly for them rather than simply act in
support roles as 'fixers' or translators. It is particularly acute for global services
addressing international audiences.

But if there are advantages to using local staff, there are also issues to
address – including safety. They may be more vulnerable to political pressure
or intimidation. The International News Safety Institute has calculated that on
average two journalists a week are killed doing their job – the vast majority
of them local journalists and most of those murdered for investigating crime
or corruption.[104] Local staff may be subject to social or political pressures that
outsiders are not; simply by virtue of living in a local community they may be
less inclined to report critically about their home country.

Local journalists will inevitably be directly affected by the issues they
report in a way 'foreign' correspondents are not. Melanie Bunce examined
the reporting of the Kenyan protests by local staff within the Reuters Nairobi
Bureau.

> *Many of the Kenyans in the newsroom had very strong
> political and personal feelings on the crisis itself, and they
> found it difficult to remain impartial. Cracks emerged
> between those who supported ODM and those who supported
> Kibaki. (Patrick) Muiruri described the tension: 'It was
> completely obvious that everyone was on different sides. I'm
> Kikuyu, and my mother rang me up in tears – my aunt's
> house was burnt down. So I'm angry, and I want to write
> a big critical rant about ODM. But then, another guy here
> is talking to me and his friend's house is burnt down on the
> other side … my job was to kind of try and find a balance
> between that but it was very hard.'[105]*

[103] Email interview with author, March 2010.
[104] www.newssafety.com/stories/insi/killingthemessenger.htm.
[105] M. Bunce, '"This Place Used to Be a White British Boys' Club": Reporting Dynamics and Cultural Clash at
an International News Bureau in Nairobi', *The Round Table: Commonwealth Journal of International Affairs*,
99/410 (2010), 523.

In spite of the many advantages to increasing use of local staff, there are potential disadvantages and significant issues which news organisations need to manage both on behalf of the staff and the quality of service they seek to offer.

News agendas

There is also the question of their ability to communicate across cultures. The need to explain the interdependence of the world grows, but cultural gulfs are still wide and most audiences are more interested in local issues than global ones. The role of cultural bridge is of growing not lessening importance and cannot always be achieved by indigenous reporters. For all the virtues of employing local staff for an informed local perspective, the outsider's view remains essential too. Distance provides perspective.

Ethan Zuckerman explains it like this:

> *I think there's something very powerful about framing an international news story for a local audience. In the same way that I celebrate bridge figures who blog for their ability to reframe local issues for a global context. I think foreign correspondents are often a critical bridge, providing context and translation that makes a story in India important and comprehensible to an audience in Illinois.*[106]

For national newspapers or broadcasters, an understanding of the readership or audience 'at home' is seen as crucial to much international coverage. And most national news organisations still believe an expatriate correspondent is best placed to do that. The question is whether that will remain the case as audiences become more diverse and globalisation continues to affect the news agenda, blurring distinctions between home and foreign news.

Lucila Vargas and Lisa Paulin have proposed the term 'transnational news' to span the blurring of the old foreign and domestic divide:

> *Technologies have dramatically changed the gathering, production and distribution of foreign news but ... they have also been critical in the development of new publics and new subjects or beats for what can be called 'transnational affairs' reporting ... Diasporic people develop bicultural identities or a sense of belonging to more than one setting. For many, information about the homeland is as relevant and familiar as news about their present place of residence.*[107]

---

[106] Interview with author, March 2010.
[107] L. Vargas and L. Paulin, *Rethinking Foreign News from a Transnational Perspective: From Pigeons to News Portals* (LSU, 2007).

For many diaspora communities in the West, news of Asia is home news. Climate change is both local and global. The geopolitical environment, the openness of communications, global trade and economics and social mobility all have an impact on the news agenda.

Reuters' Sean Maguire explains:

> *Globalisation has fundamentally affected how the world works. It has changed enormously societies, economies, trading patterns and balances of power. If we are to recognise the world as it is, with all its challenges, how could what is reported not change? There are still plenty of parochial and narrow-minded news organisations who make a decent living recycling a hackneyed outlook on the world. But even they can't ignore that their audience now travels routinely to parts of Eastern Europe that were off limits 20 years ago and buys houses there, purchases Chinese-made electronics without qualms and takes long-distance air travel for granted.[108]*

This has consequences for how newsdesks organise their coverage. The framework that delivered news in the context of the Cold War may not be appropriate for a more open, interconnected world. And cultural assumptions about the audience or readership of 20 years ago won't hold true today.

In the days of the Cold War there was a clear narrative which provided a simple lens through which to see international events. The end of the Cold War and globalisation, and the cultural changes it is bringing, have complicated the framework for international news.

Media columnist William Powers:

> *Foreign news is out there in great profusion these days, particularly online, but it is a different kind of foreign news. While the old foreign news had an air of urgency that was a product of the cold war and technological constraints, the new foreign news is diffuse, many-layered, sprawling, chaotic and terribly complicated ... like the world itself.[109]*

Tom Kent of the AP has noted how the end of the Cold War left many Americans with no framework for international news.

---

[108] Interview with author, Feb. 2010.
[109] William Powers, 'Hello World', *National Journal*, 33/26 (2001), 2082.

In the past, if there had been a war between the Hutu and
the Tutsi our first question would have been, 'who is ours and
who is theirs?' And there was a likelihood that one side or the
other would have been getting arms and support from one of
the main camps in the Cold War and the other side from the
opposite camp. Now it is not as simple as 'us and them'.[110]

In this environment it is easy to see how the old structures of international newsgathering may no longer be adequate to report the fluidity and connectedness of the modern world. Old structures and approaches risk delivering news that is less relevant to a mobile, connected, interracial public.

The issues at stake are partly professional – how best to serve news consumers, how best to run newsgathering operations – but also moral. How should we try to understand and represent other countries and peoples who are physically distant from us?

Perspectives

One problem of course is that audiences in different parts of the world may have a very different view of events. Ibrahim Helal has experience of different audiences working for Al Jazeera and for the BBC:

For example the execution of Saddam Hussein was seen in
most of the Arab world as a crime and an illegal killing. In
Kuwait it was seen as delayed victory for the invasion of
the country in 1990, in Kurds areas and Iran it was seen as
an action of justice. In Austria it was criticised as an illegal
killing but in the USA was seen as a victory. If you talk about
other less politicised events like natural disasters, most of
the societies and cultures see them less differently. Religious
societies may consider earthquakes as a punishment from
God!

These differences are less pronounced for specialist news. As the *FT* has gone global in its distribution, their CEO John Ridding believes only minor adjustments to local perspectives are needed:

We do not want to editiorialise too much because our
audience is international. A banker in New York is interested
in the same issues as a banker in Stockholm or Singapore.
The front pages in online are tailored a bit to the region but

---

[110] Quoted in U. Hannerz, *Foreign News* (2004), 25.

*you'll find pretty much all of the articles in the Europe edition
in the Asia and US edition.[111]*

No single organisation can encompass every global viewpoint. So some focus on serving particular political or cultural perspectives and abandon the idea of impartiality or reject the opportunity of a global audience. Fox News serves a politically right-wing audience; Al Jazeera Arabic seeks to serve the Arab street. Most readerships or audiences have a local or national point of reference which they expect their news provider to recognise.

However, the last decade has seen exponential growth in the number of international news services offering a range of different viewpoints. Most are state-funded to present a particular perspective on global events – Russia Today, France 24, Telesur, Iran's Press TV, Al Jazeera and more. They are often seeking to break what they perceive as a Western grip on global news, information and debate, and very much seeking to address the 'supply' side.[112]

Alternatively others, including the BBC and CNN, hope that providing a platform for a wide range of opinions can reassure people across the political spectrum and maintain a sense of impartiality and independence. So the BBC increasingly offers the opportunity for the audiences across the globe to contribute through international programmes like *World Have Your Say*.[113]

Blogs and social media may help. They are not only useful as 'canaries in the mine shaft', providing early warning of events or firsthand witnessing. They are also important in communicating attitudes which may differ from our own.

When Chinese blogs expressed anger before the Beijing Olympics at Western protests about Chinese management of the torch relay it was less about Western attitudes to human rights, and more because they believed the West was jealous about the rise of China as a global power. It was a clear example of the clash of values between East and West, where China believed national unity and pride to be more important than an issue of human rights in Tibet – which received concerted coverage by Western news organisations.

Similarly, as much of the West reported Iranian protests in 2009 via Twitter and YouTube, the Farsi blogs reflected much stronger conservative support for Ahmadinejad and the widely held belief that the protests were orchestrated by the West. Social media are called social for a reason – they reflect a deeper and wider range of attitudes in society, of interest to anyone engaged with those parts of the world.

[111] Quoted in Currah, *What's Happening*, 112.
[112] See James Painter, *Counter-Hegemonic News*:
http://reutersinstitute.politics.ox.ac.uk/nc/publications/risj-challenges/counter-hegemonic-news.html.
[113] A daily global phone-in programme which takes comments from around the world on a set topic.

Maria Balinska, a former BBC editor, puts it this way:

> *International coverage too often fails to reflect – or
> take advantage of – the increasing networks of personal
> relationships that globalisation enables. The ease and
> familiarity of these global connections speak, however, to
> the potential of a bottom–up approach to international
> journalism. … Historically, foreign affairs journalism has
> taken its cue from governmental priorities; war, trade policy,
> disaster relief. It's past time to expand its focus – to welcome
> the grassroots perspectives of ordinary people.*[114]

Interactivity and engagement with diverse audiences is increasingly important in all areas of reporting – including international news. The traditional news disciplines of impartiality and objectivity are proving less robust in a heavily interconnected and diverse public space and are challenged by the depth and range of views now available. A 'bottom–up' agenda may not reflect traditional Western news values but be centred on issues of more local relevance. Greater transparency about how and why news judgements are reached will be necessary to retain public trust.

Conclusion

- There are increasing pressures on news organisations to ensure their staff and structures of newsgathering reflect the changing, multicultural world. Most coverage is now accessible globally.

- This provides greater incentives to employ local staff overseas, who can provide instant expertise and cultural context. But there are risks to employing local staff as well as advantages – particularly safety and intimidation.

- Local staff need to learn the skills to report and communicate with international readers and audiences – cultural bridging is growing in importance as international news resources shrink.

- International and domestic news agendas are merging, raising structural issues about how news coverage is

[114] M. Balinska, 'It's the Audience, Stupid!', *Nieman Reports*, Sept 2010.

organised to reflect the interconnectedness of the world.

- Some news outlets are more nationalistic in the face of global exposure, others seek a global audience and agenda.

- A more 'bottom–up' international agenda is emerging, with greater interactivity available to global audiences.

- Global differences in cultural values and agendas are being revealed more than ever before posing challenges to transnational news services.

Such changes beg the question – more than ever – about what audiences actually want in terms of international news.

5. The Public Appetite for Foreign News

It has long been a tenet of news editing that people aren't interested in foreign news. In the West, magazines apparently sell fewer copies with a foreign news story on the cover, fewer people stay with the TV or radio news when it is dominated by foreign news, outside of an extreme crisis.

Yet, as we have seen, globalisation is merging the foreign and domestic news agendas. What happens abroad has a greater direct impact on lives than ever before. Global terror is a domestic issue in the USA and Europe; what happens in Asia is home news for diaspora communities across the West; climate change is a global problem with local effects; the performance of the Chinese economy can directly affect jobs and pensions in the UK or the USA. The world is more interconnected than ever.

There is a strong public interest argument in informing people about the rest of the world – often put forward by academics, politicians and media professionals. The DFiD report on international coverage in UK television in 2007 is typical:

> As globalisation and migration require us to interact with other cultures, and our economic, political and social interdependence with other countries becomes ever more apparent, so there is a growing need for UK citizens to have a greater awareness and understanding of the wider world and their place in it[115]

But in spite of this imperative, do the public want to be taught about remote events and issues a long way from their front door? Do they really need to know about international policy issues?

Journalistic experience suggests they are less interested in top–down international agendas but respond strongly to crisis, drama and human

---

[115] www.dfid.gov.uk/pubs/files/screeningreport-020608.pdf.

interest. So stories like the rescue of 33 trapped Chilean miners in October 2010 merit huge coverage over several days. Or during the Haiti earthquake, CNN deliberately focused on human drama with presenters personally rescuing a boy from mob violence and their (qualified) medical correspondent carrying out operations on victims on air. For some this seems to cross any boundary of journalistic independence. But it was compelling viewing. Climate change talks, on the other hand, in spite of huge global significance, seem to merit at best a lukewarm public response. This leads to confusion over the genuine level of interest in international events and issues.

By comparing a range of public research studies on attitudes to international news[116] in the UK and USA it is possible to identify some consistent themes among Western audiences. This research is primarily concerned with broadcast news – TV is still the primary source of news in developed countries.

Overall interest in international news

First, understanding what's going on in the world remains one of the main reasons why audiences follow the news – in some surveys it is the main reason. In Ofcom's 2007 study, 70 per cent of respondents said it was their main motivation, ahead of any other – a figure confirmed in a BBC survey in 2010.[117] Even the majority of younger audiences follow the news to understand what's happening in the world.

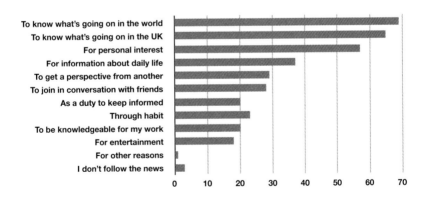

Figure 5.1. Reasons for following the news (Ofcom, *New News, Future News,* 2007)

[116] Studies compared: Ofcom, *New News, Future News* (2007): http://stakeholders.ofcom.org.uk/market-data-research/tv-research/newnews/; S. Barnett, E. Seymour and I. Gaber, *From Callaghan to Kosovo* (University of Westminster, 2000): www.ofcom.org.uk/static/archive/itc/research/callaghan_to-kosovo.pdf; various reports from Pew Research Centre 1986–2010; BBC internal audience research 2010; Media Standards Trust, *Brave New World* (2010); Tyndall Report (www.tyndallreport.com); YouGov, *What the World Thinks* (2010).
[117] The BBC internal research was part of their regular PULSE survey conducted in Aug. 2010 and based on a sample size of 1,391.

Three-quarters of all those surveyed in the UK by Ofcom said it was the most important public purpose for broadcasting. However, a quarter of all audiences and a third of under 25s claim to be bored by it[118] and interest in specific domestic and local news stories tends to be higher than interest in international stories.[119]

Demographic breakdown on international news interest

More affluent and better educated audiences show a higher interest in international news compared to less affluent groups. Ofcom's research showed interest levels almost double in the higher AB group than C2s or DEs.

	Total (2216)	AB (340)	C1 (614)	C2 (459)	DE (803)
Current events in the UK	55%	70%	54%	53%	44%
Current events in my region*	50%	59%	46%	53%	44%
Current local events where I live	48%	52%	45%	48%	45%
Weather	48%	55%	51%	45%	42%
Crime	47%	45%	46%	51%	48%
World wide politics and current events	41%	61%	42%	30%	31%
Sports	39%	41%	40%	40%	34%
Human interest stories	38%	42%	34%	42%	36%
UK-wide politics	37%	55%	38%	28%	25%
Entertainment	34%	32%	36%	32%	36%
Politics in my region*	28%	36%	27%	24%	24%
Travel	26%	31%	26%	25%	22%
Consumer affairs	23%	32%	23%	18%	19%
City, business and financial issues	19%	30%	19%	15%	12%
Celebrity behaviour	13%	11%	14%	12%	14%

* 'My region' is replaced with Scotland, Wales, Northern Island in those nations. Unweighed bases in brackets.

Figure 5.2. Interest in news topics by socio-economic group (Ofcom, *New News, Future News*, 2007)

In the USA, Pew's research shows more than twice the levels of knowledge among college graduates compared to other groups.[120] And there is a gender gap, with men having a significantly higher interest in international affairs than women in both the UK and the USA. Ethnic minority groups, particularly black African and Asian audiences, have a higher interest than white audiences – reflecting their ethnic roots and extended family connections around the world.

Interest in specific stories

Although the interest in international news is high, the engagement in individual international stories tends to be more fragmented. BBC research shows higher levels of interest for global-themed coverage such as terrorism,

[118] BBC audience research, 2010.
[119] *New News, Future News.*
[120] Pew, *What Americans Know* (1989–2007).

economics and climate change than for specific country coverage – reflecting a merging of the international and domestic news agenda.

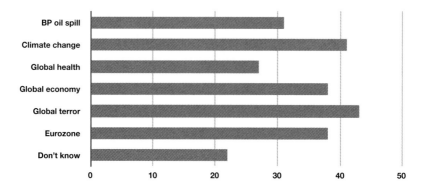

Figure 5.3. 'Which stories will you follow closely in next few years?' (BBC, Aug. 2010)

The top three issues for UK audiences were the economy, crime and immigration – the first and third of which have strong global narratives, essential to a full understanding of the issue.

International accidents and disasters tend to spike interest rather than ongoing conflicts or extended issues. The reporting of the Haiti earthquake in January 2010 produced some of the highest levels of engagement among BBC audiences. Outside of the election and the BP oil spill, interest in the USA was below average. Iran was very closely followed during the 2009 election, but much less so since. The conflict in Gaza at the end of 2008 was by some measure more closely followed than any other Israeli/Palestinian development. For UK audiences the troop deaths and equipment issues in Afghanistan have meant that story was consistently more closely followed than most.

This reinforces the sense that there is a low and fragmented level of interest in individual countries – but acute moments of crisis can attract significant attention.

Twenty-two per cent say they will closely follow the rise of China over the next few years, compared with 25 per cent for Iran and 13 per cent for developments in Africa. Interest in the BRIC countries generally is low – although clearly there is a question over whether the significance of these economies has been sufficiently explained to arouse serious interest and engagement.[121]

---

[121] BBC internal audience research.

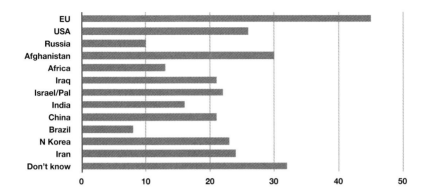

Figure 5.4. Interest in following news from particular countries, 1986–2006 (BBC, Aug. 2010)

The Pew News Interest index looking at what news the US public follows over ten years from 1986 to 2007 put disaster coverage at 39 per cent compared with 17 per cent for foreign news in general.

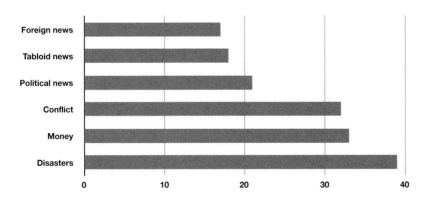

Figure 5.5. Interest in six combined news categories 1986–2007 (BBC, Aug. 2010)

Although this figure changes according to the importance of events in the news, no shift is detected with the proliferation of channels. In other words, the arrival of 24-hour TV news and then the internet has not deepened the American public's levels of interest in news overall. US foreign policy or news about other nations scored significantly lower than average for Americans – although ahead of celebrity scandal.[122]

---

[122] Pew, News Interest Index 1986–2007.

Treatment of stories

Across all age groups, UK audiences (close to two-thirds) say they value seeing correspondents reporting directly from the country where the story is taking place – reinforcing the importance of eyewitness reporting. Just under half of them appreciate getting a perspective from another country.

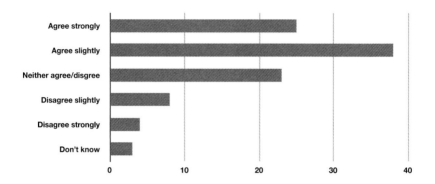

Figure 5.6. Important correspondent reports from country where story is happening (BBC, Aug. 2010)

Having a familiar accent does increase the likelihood of audiences engaging in a story, however, if UK reporters are unavailable at the scene they are satisfied with local commentary – translated if necessary.[123] This suggests their tolerance for local reporters may be higher than assumed.

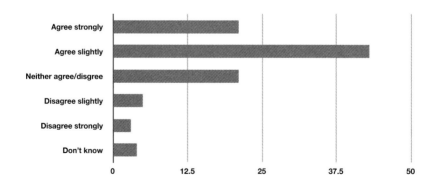

Figure 5.7. Satisfied with local commentary of live event if UK reporter unavailable (BBC, Aug. 2010)

[123] BBC internal audience research.

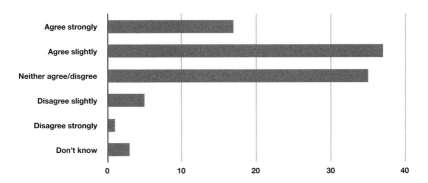

Figure 5.8. Prefer to hear from reporter who is expert in the country rather than general reporter flown in (BBC, Aug. 2010)

The public are able to separate the national importance of stories from the personal importance. A YouGov survey[124] showed 17 per cent believed Afghanistan was one of the most important issues facing the country – but only 2 per cent of them believed it was one of the most important issues facing their family. Again this suggests a recognition of the public-interest importance of international news above purely personal interest.

Audiences are evenly divided on whether news is only trustworthy when the events have been witnessed by reporters themselves – suggesting it is the news provider's brand rather than story treatment which drives trust. But they do value a country expert reporting from abroad rather than a general reporter, recognising the importance of specialism or expertise.

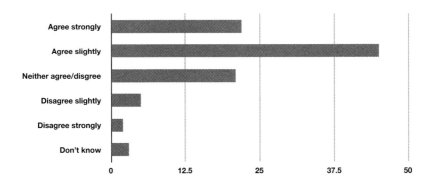

Figure 5.9. Interest in material from ordinary people caught up in events (BBC, Aug. 2010)

[124] *What the World Thinks* (2010).

They are very interested in seeing material from ordinary people caught up in events (68 per cent saying this would increase their interest in a story) – reinforcing that citizen journalism and human interest are strong motivations to engage with the news. [125]

Conclusions

These findings are restricted to the UK and the USA and subject to the caveats surrounding all audience research – they are merely indicative of what those questioned say they believe. However, there are consistent findings.

- There is clear recognition of the importance of international news and of personal value in finding out what's happened in the world.

- International news is expected to be an integral part of any serious news offer.

- The more affluent and better educated demographics show greater interest in foreign affairs – leading to a potential knowledge divide about the rest of the world.

- Interest and understanding may be driven by news coverage – areas which are little covered in the UK, for example, excite little interest even when they may be economically significant like Brazil or China.

- It is possible to see in this the potential self-reinforcing, downward spiral in terms of news coverage and public interest and understanding of global issues. This supports the arguments of those who believe the shrinking of international news coverage could have a detrimental social impact. However, providing a global context to national stories of interest does appear to be an opportunity to redress this to some extent.

- Interest in foreign news is fragmenting (as it is in all other categories of news) with deep niche interest in some subjects and cursory or 'headline' interest beyond those areas. This supports the loss of the 'middle ground' in international coverage and the shift of resources by news

[125] BBC internal audience research.

organisations towards breaking news and depth and analysis. The foreign feature coverage, which sustained correspondents and bureaux in the past appears to be little valued by audiences. Crises still provoke the highest levels of engagement by a significant margin.

- Finally the higher levels of interest among some ethnic groups supports the view that multicultural mixed societies may require a differently balanced news agenda. And even beyond those groups, there is an acceptance of local reporters to a higher degree than editors may have assumed – although still a preference for correspondents who can culturally bridge between international events and the domestic audience.

6. On the Ground: Introducing the Case Studies

We have seen how a range of forces are affecting the structures and routines of international reporting and the assumptions that have lain behind it for the last hundred years. In the West and developed countries, expensive foreign bureaux have closed, the quantity of international coverage has shrunk and there is much talk of journalism in crisis. At the same time, technology, both within and outside the news industry, is providing many opportunities for new approaches to reporting the world. The cultural changes brought about by globalisation are bringing new pressures to bear on how news organisations approach foreign coverage – particularly those with international readerships or audiences – and also how they portray foreign events and people.

The 'crisis' in journalism is very much a Western one – centred in the USA and Europe. In other parts of the world, news is booming. There are dozens of news channels and new print titles launched in India – some now looking to extend themselves overseas.[126] Billions of dollars of investment are going into China's international news services. New internet opportunities, of the kind often accused of undermining Western news services, are providing African countries with a growing opportunity to develop their journalism and influence how Africa is seen by the rest of the world.

Technology and an increased reliance on local journalists is helping Western correspondents report difficult countries like Iran or China better – but still with real limits on what they can offer, how far they can bridge cultural divides, and the political and social pressures to which they are exposed.

The pressures changing foreign reporting for Western news organisations are felt differently in other parts of the world. And that in turn is affecting how the West reports them.

---

[126] India's TV9 is looking to launch in Africa and offers vernacular news in the USA: www.businessworld.in/index.php/Media-Entertainment/The-Lead-Story.html.

The following sections consider three very different examples: China, Africa and Iran.

7. China: The Dragon Stirs

Seek Truth from facts (Deng Xiaoping)

In October 2009, 300 delegates from more than 170 media organisations around the world walked into the Great Hall of the People in Beijing for what the Chinese authorities called the World Media Summit. On stage with Chinese President Hu Jintao were leaders of 12 global news organisations.[127] They listened as the Chinese President urged the world's media to accept social responsibility, help build relations between countries and work for peace. He also said he would support the rights of foreign news media and further facilitate coverage of China.

It was an occasion which illustrated both sides of the conundrum of international news and China. On the one hand, it was a demonstration of China's growing confidence on the world stage, in media as in other areas, being seen to convene international leaders at Beijing's table. It coincided with huge investment in Xinhua, the official Chinese news agency, to spread its wings with new international services and bureaux around the world to project China's voice more loudly in the global media arena. It was a speech thick with 'Asian Values' of social harmony, partnership, concern for welfare over rights and respect for authority.

On the other hand, for international media figures, it was an opportunity to explore new ways to serve the huge Chinese market, and to report what is happening in a fast-growing superpower where reporting has always been difficult.

The event achieved more for China than for the international media. Unlike the West, China is expanding its international journalism, from America to Zimbabwe, albeit with significant state funding. In 2009 the Chinese government announced that it will spend almost $7 billion on the international

---

[127] Including myself representing the BBC. As Director of Global News I was among 12 international news executives invited to be alongside the President of Xinhua 'hosting' the summit.

expansion of key domestic media outlets, of which $2.2 billion will be spent each on CCTV and the Xinhua news agency: a stark contrast to the pressures on international resources felt by even public-funded Western media.

They are creating new English-language TV networks, pouring millions into newspapers, leasing radio stations and syndicating content across the world, and broadcasting TV news to a worldwide audience in six languages. The Xinhua news agency has moved into new offices in Times Square in New York. What was a print agency is being equipped and trained to report back in TV and the web through a network of 200 bureaus around the world. CCTV, China's state TV network, is planning to grow from 10 bureaux to about 50 worldwide – just for English-language services. And they are backing this up with ambitious programmes of journalism training.[128]

It is an attempt to improve China's image around the world. Wang Chen, the head of the party's overseas propaganda division, said the media should boost 'capacity to broadcast, to positively influence international public opinion and to establish a good image for our nation'.[129] While the impact may not yet be felt in the West, for the developing world, China is emerging as a significant global information provider.[130]

There is growth in China's indigenous media as well – mostly fuelled commercially. In 2009, China's media industry grew year on year to 491 billion yuan ($72 billion), growth of 16 per cent. This included operating revenue from newspaper advertisements bucking the global trend, and increasing by 8 per cent to 37 billion yuan.[131]

This has been fed by a commercial approach to expansion. Even subsidies to the *People's Daily* have been reduced and its costs are now supported by the commercial profits of the *Global Times* – a highly successful brash tabloid paper.

A shift in media policy was signalled in a key speech in 2008 by Li Changchun, the party leader responsible for propaganda, in which he said: 'In the modern age, whichever nation's communication methods are most advanced, whichever nations communication capacity is strongest … has the most power to influence the world.'[132] While close internal controls continue, the party has made a strategic decision in terms of how China should be perceived around the world.

He Dalong, the London Bureau Chief of Xinhua confirms the changes underway.

---

[128] www.atimes.com/atimes/China/KI04Ad01.html.

[129] wwwforeignpolicy.com/articles/2009/05/14/we_report_we_decide.

[130] See Chan Yuen-Ying, 'A Scholar's View: The State Media have an Iron Grip and Grand Plans', *Global Asia*, 22 June 2010.

[131] www.ipsnews.net/print.asp?idnews=50739.

[132] http://cmp.hku.hk/2009/01/19/1457/.

There has been a big change since 2008 when there was a new strategy for Xinhua – to have more and more people around the world use us, and to go multimedia – text, photographs and video. When I was Washington correspondent 25 years ago I just did text interviews. Today my job is to manage multimedia coverage.[133]

He says Xinhua is involved in two paths – to tell the Chinese people what is going on in the world but also to tell the world what is going on in China – as part of China's 'Open Door' policy.[134]

Telling the world about China however remains challenging for Western foreign correspondents. Carrie Gracie was the BBC's Beijing correspondent in the early 1990s and regularly returns to report from China. She says part of the problem for Western news organisations is matching daily news agendas to the scale of change underway.

We see tiny incremental changes each day which are part of a vast change. It's difficult to find that precise tipping point to tell the bigger story. London now has an idea what it wants out of China based on a template of what everyone thinks China's place in the world will be. But it's not based on a historical narrative. China is so profoundly inside its own history and on its own historical journey, that doesn't fit in the dimensions of daily news.[135]

The bureaucracy of reporting China has improved but not gone away. It now varies according to the story. For the Sichuan earthquake in 2008, initial controls on media access were temporarily relaxed when the authorities realised publicity would show they were responding well and help bring in aid. But access to Xinjiang when there was rioting the following year was very tightly controlled. Western media were banned from Tibet during protests in 2008 as well.

CBS correspondent Barry Petersen puts it this way:

The first thing you need to know about your rights as a foreign reporter in China is that in the end you have no rights. Yes they have books of rules and regulations, but the only rules that count are the ones made up by the policeman or foreign ministry officer sitting in front of you.[136]

[133] Interview with author, June 2010.
[134] http://news.bbc.co.uk/1/shared/spl/hi/asia_pac/02/china_party_congress/china_ruling_party/key_people_events/html/open_door_policy.stm.
[135] Interview with author, July 2010.
[136] CBS, *Public Eye*, 26 April 2006.

There is still, of course, significant political control of Chinese media. Richard McGregor, former Beijing correspondent of the *FT* describes it as the propaganda department channelling rather than controlling news. 'It's like rivulets of water running down a window. There may be many different ones to begin with but they can all be brought together.'[137]

Manuel Castells has described it as institutionalised self-censorship: 'the cascading hierarchy of surveillance that ultimately induces self-censorship at all levels and makes the culprit pay at each level when a significant failure of control is detected.'[138]

Channel 4 News correspondent, Lindsey Hilsum, recalls going to the Sichuan earthquake.

> *No Chinese journalists were officially allowed to go at first, but the story was so enormous many of them just went anyway. One of them told me 'I have to be here and if they spike my story I'll just be a volunteer'. Within a day it had all changed and Chinese TV was running 24 hour live coverage. Then the real story got out – schools had collapsed because they were so badly built as corrupt officials had pocketed the construction funds – and it all clamped down again and some Chinese journalists were imprisoned.*[139]

Reuters Editor-in-Chief David Schlesinger however sees a big change. From his time as Bureau Chief in Beijing and then editor of the region for Reuters he believes people speak more openly now than in the past. Reuters has significantly increased staffing in Beijing, largely with local staff. 'They are fully trained by us and contribute fully to our reporting.'[140]

One of the difficulties for many Western correspondents in China is that they don't speak the language or know the culture well. Carrie Gracie believes many news organisations have failed to train up for China in order to have staff with the skills to report the scale of change. 'If you have no language, no sources, no context, even if you are a great story-teller, you are going to struggle.'

This undoubtedly contributes to the perception among many in China that Western coverage is unfair or biased against them. Rebecca MacKinnon quotes one Chinese blogger who was uncomfortable after being interviewed by the BBC:

---

[137] Interview with author, Aug. 2010.
[138] M. Castells, *Communication Power* (2009), 283.
[139] RISJ seminar.
[140] Interview with author, July 2010.

> *The problem I see besides the two worlds are, there are too many pre-defined questions like censorship and BBC is trying to find piece of information, filter it, and create an exciting picture for people in the 'civilised' world ... The reason I was not comfortable with the interview is not talking about censorship. The problem is I don't want to be put into a condition that there is a pre-set conclusion and my role is just to act as a victim in the story and confirm it. (Wang JianShuo)*[141]

Part of this is a clash of editorial cultures. Many Western journalists concentrate on human rights and centralised political control as a core agenda. From a Chinese perspective, social welfare and development may be more important. So Western news organisations don't report China the way its population perceive it. And the Chinese don't always cooperate with a Western news agenda.

Vincent Ni, a past researcher at the Oxford Internet Institute, worked as an assistant to Western TV correspondents in Beijing.

> *Most Foreign journalists just want to know what the audience at home would be interested in. They would tell me the kind of story they wanted and I would do some research, talk to friends, go online and find contacts for them. I go to blogs to find out what's going on, as China-based foreign journalists are now more and more keen on 'public opinion' expressed by internet users. I also read blogs written by Chinese journalists as some will write the official version and then blog what they really think.*[142]

He added that many Chinese journalists, among others, would not express criticism of China to foreign journalists as it was seen as unpatriotic.

The language barrier, cultural gulf, complexity of the China story and deeply established templates for stories about China (in this case the problem of censorship) all contribute to the perception of unfair or ill-informed coverage. However, immense social change is underway – again partly facilitated by technology. China is online and mobile. There are nearly 550 million mobile phone users[143] and 384 million internet users – most of them on broadband.[144]

---

[141] Quoted in R. MacKinnon, *Flatter World and Thicker Walls? Blogs, Censorship and Civic Discourse in China* (Berkman Center, 2008).
[142] Interview with author, June 2010.
[143] www.telecomasia.net/content/chinas-mobile-phone-penetration-rate-reaches-416-0.
[144] www.internetworldstats.com/asia.htm.

A recent study of media usage by Chinese youth shows the internet beats TV, print and radio in all social groups apart from in rural areas, but there, mobile is the most used medium.[145]

This has opened up the public space. 'The amount of public discussion which has moved out of central control is immense', says Carrie Gracie. And public opinion is being felt over issues like the tainted baby milk in 2008.[146] 'The more those kinds of issue surface, the more they will recognise the importance of free media.'

There was a significant public and political backlash against the media and regional powers who suppressed news of the Sanlu baby milk contamination in the run-up to the Olympics.

> *For reasons that everybody knows, we were not able to investigate the Sanlu case because (pre Olympics) harmony was needed everywhere. I was deeply concerned because I sensed that this was going to be a huge public health catastrophe but I could not send reporters to investigate. (Fu Jianfeng of the Southern Weekend newspaper)[147]*

But as Richard McGregor writes, any public outcry was quickly stifled by the party:

> *Party bodies censored the news, usurped the management of the company, sidelined the board, and finally sacked and arrested the executives. When the victims mobilised to take legal action, party bodies intimidated lawyers, manipulated the courts and bought off the litigants before finally letting a handful of cases proceed.[148]*

According to Xinhua, two men were later executed for their part in the scandal.[149]

Although the party's control of damaging protest and reporting is still tight, he agrees that there is a burgeoning 'rights' culture in the Chinese public, largely fed by property issues. He once asked a question at a press conference about property rights – and a year later was still getting calls from people in remote provinces asking for his help. Journalism is thriving in China, he says, and commercialisation has helped.

---

[145] Synovate Media Atlas, China, Dec. 2009–Feb. 2010.
[146] www.time.com/time/world/article/0,8599,1841535,00.html.
[147] McGregor, *The Party* (2010), 170.
[148] Ibid.
[149] http://news.xinhuanet.com/english/2009-11/24/content_12530798.htm.

Mainstream media is becoming more professional and more sophisticated – including investigative journalism – but as Haiyan Wang concluded in her study of 'Investigative Journalism and Political Power in China':

> *Media marketisation has to some extent undermined the power of politics but is far from having fundamentally disrupted it. China's thirty-year media reform merely offered a new bottle (marketisation) for the old wine (political control). Politics still takes the lead in the media–politics relationship. One major difference from the old master-servant model is that the political parties now not only shout orders but also give treats. Controlling political and economic resources and delivering them to the media in exchange for support and loyalty, forces media and politics into a clientelistic relationship. In turn, the media serve their political patrons with obsequious journalism and the subsequent favourable public influence to trade for the opportunity of surviving in the tight political atmosphere and the profitable marketplace.[150]*

Caijing magazine had seemed to be an exception. An investigative magazine it broke new ground by exposing corruption, public health issues and other sensitive topics. It enjoyed a level of support from senior political leaders which allowed it to survive for ten years before its editor and more than 60 staff resigned in 2009 in an argument with its publisher over editorial control.

It distinguished itself by refusing to allow staff to accept the 'red envelopes' or payoffs common in other parts of Chinese media. Such payoffs are systematised – with agreed levels of payment – and becoming more entrenched. As the *FT*'s Richard McGregor put it:

> *With commercialisation comes corruption. What's the most important trend, the growth of genuine journalism or the wholesale perversion of values that's come with that growth? That's the kind of question you can ask about China generally. Is the glass half full or half empty?[151]*

However, with significant online growth, is the new public space online providing better information for those wishing to report the real changes in China? The first point to note is that the online community anywhere, but

---

[150] http://reutersinstitute.politics.ox.ac.uk/fileadmin/documents/Publications/Working_Papers/Investigative_Journalism_and_Political_Power_in_China.pdf.
[151] Interview with author, Aug. 2010.

including China, is not representative of the public as a whole – merely of the usually more affluent, educated demographic who choose to engage online.

But unquestionably the growth of social media has become a source of more candid information for foreign correspondents. Blogs and social media are not monitored in real time, and even if self-regulation is still at work, more candid information is available online.

Rebecca MacKinnon notes:

> *The advent of the internet in China – and the emergence by the late 1990s of spaces where Chinese people endeavoured to speak candidly (if anonymously) online – was a very welcome development for China correspondents, given the myriad challenges they face in gathering reliable information about what is happening around the country and what the Chinese public really thinks. By 2000 Internet chatrooms had grown sufficiently large and popular that foreign journalists, often encouraged by their local staff, began following and reporting on key online discussions – especially during times of crisis and media crackdowns.[152]*

In a survey she conducted at the Foreign Correspondents Club in China, 90 per cent of respondents said they used blogs as a source of news.[153] Among those used, ESWN, authored by Hong Kong media analyst Roland Soong, was seen as particularly valuable for translating between Mandarin and English and providing first reports in English of a number of stories originating in Chinese on the internet. Among these was a 2005 bus explosion in the city of Fuzhou, and a legal argument between two Chinese reporters and iPod subcontractor Foxcomm in which Soong admitted to using his research and translation skills to 'lobby, persuade and bully the western media to pick up the story'.[154]

MacKinnon concludes that, however vibrant the Chinese online community may be, it takes 'bridge-bloggers' like Soong to ensure such stories are discovered in the West: bloggers 'with some professional credentials, ability to access or locate original information of interest to broader audiences and a sophisticated understanding of how media works'.[155]

The role of a Western foreign correspondent in China has always been challenging. Tight controls on access, tightly controlled official media,

---

[152] R. MacKinnon, 'Blogs and China Correspondence: Lessons about Global Information Flow', University of Hong Kong 2008.
[153] Ibid.
[154] Soong, 'My Life as an Active Journalist', www.zonaeuropa.com/20060831_1.htm.
[155] Ibid.

internet censorship and filtering as well as the deeper issues of language and cultural barriers all contribute to making it hard to reflect the profound changes underway.

There is a continuing clash between Asian values, where the media is a project of the state and largely expected to promote social stability, and Western news values, where the media is expected to hold power to account. Human and civil rights simply do not hold the same position in Chinese culture or media as they do in the West. As China, and Chinese media, expand, that clash is likely to become more stark.

However, the growing public space online, combined with 'bridge bloggers' and others, is making it easier than ever to probe beneath the surface of Chinese society. News organisations need to train staff to understand China, take advantage of the increasing number of young, educated Chinese who are able to report for the West and shed some of the prescriptive templates of the past to really understand what is happening.

A diverse, specialist approach is going to become increasingly important in adequately reporting the huge changes taking place – particularly given the apparently low levels of interest in China among audiences in the West. It must be one of the most crucial countries, and stories, where the role of cultural bridge is essential for correspondents.

8. Africa: Learning to Report Itself

*There was nothing new, no insight, but lots of 'reportage' –
Oh, gosh, wow, look, golly ooo – as if Africa and Africans
were not part of the conversation. (Binyavanga Wainaina[156])*

Western coverage of Africa has long been criticised for being negative and focusing on famine and war. Regular academic, charity and media conferences and reports have analysed and discussed the portrayal of the continent. The starting point is often a profound dissatisfaction with international news coverage. A conference at Cardiff University in 2009, for example, organised by a UK charity Skills For Africa set up the discussion this way:

*There is a strong perception among Africans that the western
media operates to some form of preconceived agenda – some
say conspiracy – which has as its ultimate goal the perpetual
subjugation of the continent and its peoples, wherever they
may reside. Africans point to the persistent negative portrayal
of Africa and its indigenes in news bulletins, adverts,
documentaries and features in the western media.[157]*

This view overlooks the brave and important journalism that has been conducted in Africa over many years. But whether or not this perception is fair, it is clear that Africa receives relatively little attention from Western media and the agenda is narrow. According to the Global Attention Profiles project at Harvard in 2004,[158] it is the least reported continent on earth.

Galtung and Ruge, in their seminal 1960s' study of foreign news values may have part of the explanation for this. Their analysis identified 12 factors

---

[156] http://bidoun.com/bdn/magazine/21-bazaar-ii/how-to-write-about-africa-ii-the-revenge-by-binyavanga-wainaina/.
[157] http://skillsforafrica.org/News.html.
[158] http://gapdev.law.harvard.edu/.

determining whether a country was likely to make the news and most African countries, outside times of crisis, fail on those criteria.[159]

For Western journalists there are problems of language (most reporters don't speak the local dialect), vastness (the sheer scale of the continent), lack of press freedom (when local media are usually the first source for foreign correspondents) and logistical barriers (as Ungar and Gergen put it, 'When the river crossing between Kinshasa and Brazzaville is closed the only reliable way to make that short journey may be to fly to Paris and back'[160]).

The underdeveloped media within African countries have played a part in this. Local media are crucial to international media finding out what's going on. A report at the Pan Africa Media Conference in Nairobi in 2010 suggested that indigenous African media contributed only about 2 per cent of media content on Africa.[161] Most coverage featured issues of interest to foreign investors, especially threats.

However, things may be changing. First, there are signs that mainstream news organisations are starting to take a different approach to Africa in response to economic development. Secondly, Africa's own journalistic and media capacity is increasing significantly and, thirdly, the internet and in particular the take-up of mobile phones across the continent is opening up new means of reporting and distributing information about Africa. The gatekeeper role for Western and global media is falling away in Africa as it is elsewhere.

African journalists, from bloggers, to internet aggregators and activist sites, to mainstream broadcasters and newspapers, are taking a more active role in telling the story of Africa – which in due course will shape the narrative for the rest of the world as well.

Significant investment in infrastructure in recent years has started to change the way business leaders regard Africa – and international media companies are responding. At the World Economic Summit in Davos in January 2010, the International Monetary Fund suggested growth in Sub-Saharan Africa could be a percentage point above the global average and put eight African countries in its top 20 fastest expanding economies in 2010.[162] 'Not investing in Africa is like missing out on Japan and Germany in the 1950s, Southeast Asia in the 1980s and emerging markets in the 1990s', said Francis Beddington, head of research at emerging market investment house Insparo Capital.[163]

This economic potential is underwritten by significant investment in

[159] J. Galtung, M. Ruge and M. Holmboe, 'The Structure of Foreign News: The Presentation of the Congo, Cuba and Cyprus Crises in Four Norwegian Newspapers', *Journal of Peace Research*, 2 (1965), 64–91.
[160] S. Ungar and D. Gergen, 'Africa and the American Media', Freedom Forum paper 1991.
[161] 'Leaders Pitch for a Pan African Media Outlet', *Africa Review*, 29 July 2010.
[162] www.imf.org/external/region/afr/index.htm.
[163] www.reuters.com/article/idUSTRE60P04120100126.

infrastructure from China[164] and is the backdrop to the growth in mobile phone penetration and broadband reach. The total African mobile subscriber base is expected to reach 561 million (53.5 per cent) by 2012,[165] with broadband users expected to reach 92 million by 2015.[166] Increasing political stability and improving management skills are also becoming evident according to the IMF.

This story of growth and increased political stability lay behind Reuters' decision to launch their Africa Business website, as David Schlesinger explained:

> *Whether you're talking about global terrorism, oil prices, the emergence of China, or any of the dozens of other current themes, and whether you're based in the US or anywhere else in the world, you won't get a full picture if you leave Africa out. And you can't cover Africa properly without looking at business and finance angles.[167]*

The BBC took a similar decision with the launch of *Africa Business Report*, a regular programme on BBC World News TV. The *Financial Times* runs a special section on China's interests in Africa.[168]

This doesn't, of course, mean that the problems of Darfur, Somalia, and Zimbabwe have slipped from the headlines. Nor does it mean that business and financial agendas should now dominate Western coverage. It remains essential that violence, corruption and famine should continue to be properly reported where they occur. African journalism is still dogged by political interference, corruption and intimidation. But it is also true that wider issues of economic development and the political economic and social progress being made in many countries on the continent also deserve, and are beginning to receive, greater recognition and coverage.

In large part, this is because Africa's capacity to report itself is growing. The latest (2008) IREX report for Africa shows further increases in freedom of speech and plurality of provision, but with continuing issues for professional journalism and business management. Specifically the report highlights 'weak economies and a small pool of advertisers create reliance on business or political patrons who expect positive coverage in return. In such a situation, truly independent reporting is difficult to sustain, even if a cadre of well-trained journalists exists.'[169]

[164] www.bloomberg.com/apps/news?pid=newsarchive&sid=agtnJbD9I0sA.
[165] www.mikekujawski.ca/2009/03/16/latest-mobile-phone-statistics-from-africa-and-what-this-means/.
[166] www.africagoodnews.com/ict/africa-broadband-users-to-reach-92-million-in-2015.html.
[167] http://blogs.reuters.com/reuters-editors/2007/02/26/out-of-africa/.
[168] www.ft.com/indepth/africachina.
[169] www.irex.org/programs/MSI_Africa/2008/exec.asp.

Nevertheless, there is a sense of confidence about some parts of African journalism. Wisdom J. Tetty, writing for the World Bank, reported:

> There is no question … that the media landscape in Africa over (the past twenty years) has shown significant shifts, with tremendous expansion in the number of media outlets, as democratic transformations make inroads into what used to be largely dictatorial political environments. Even countries with regimes that are not receptive to democratic ideals have not escaped these developments and have seen spaces open for mediated politics.[170]

Joel Kibazo is a Ugandan journalist who has worked for Reuters, the *FT* and the BBC:

> For so long there was no local news – you had to listen to the BBC. But the BBC has not kept up with African audiences and still talks to the Africa of 30 years ago. So they have lost audiences and lost relevance. When there are 150 radio stations in Uganda you have to offer more and speak to that audience.[171]

He said deregulation in Africa led in the immediate aftermath to a fall in editorial standards – but that is now being clawed back. Kibazo is optimistic:

> There is a new generation of qualified people becoming journalists. There is greater professionalism, more training. And African journalists are just starting to report other countries. Maybe led by Sport – but politics will follow! They are asking, for example, what the policies of the new British government will mean for Africa.

But he believes the biggest change has been the opening up of the public space, initially demanded by major aid donors in the 1990s who pushed for greater democracy. 'You couldn't open up the political space without reporting on local politics. What's this budget mean? What does this committee do? For the first time these questions were asked.'

 (Since 2008 in Kenya you can do more than ask such questions. Philip Thigo launched a Kenya budget tracking tool with cooperation from the

---

[170] Chapter in Pippa Norris (ed.), *Public Sentinel: News Media and Governance Reform* (2010).
[171] Interview with author, June 2010.

Kenyan authorities. In addition to a searchable website, it handles simple SMS queries, so that anyone with a mobile phone can text in and find out how much money has been allocated for various projects in their area. The system currently gets between 4,000 and 4,500 queries per month. Data mining made possible by the Budget Tracking Tool uncovered a major corruption scandal at the Ministry of Water that led to the firing of a number of public officials involved.[172])

The combination of more – although by no means complete – political freedom plus technology have led a raft of web services and aggregators reporting Africa to itself and to the world. The World Bank report concludes:

> *... many media outlets and journalists in Africa are fulfilling their watchdog, agenda-setting and gatekeeping roles commendably under trying circumstances. They are making tremendous contributions toward the building of democratic practices and institutions. It is also clear that the traditional media are being complemented significantly by the opportunities made possible by the internet.*

The internet is supporting two areas of development. First as a distribution network, aggregating content from across Africa and making it widely available. This is particularly important in a continent deeply segmented by language and by political restrictions at national level in many countries. Secondly, in countries where media freedom and free speech is still compromised, internet services are supporting the watchdog role of the media. Both help to open up the public space. Here are some examples.

AllAfrica.com is an online aggregator, distributing content across Africa and around the world. They claim to be 'among the Internet's largest content sites, posting over 1000 stories daily in English and French and offering a diversity of multi-lingual streaming programming as well as over 900,000 articles in our searchable archive'. CEO Reed Kramer says they use 'next-generation technology to pull, tag, index, deliver and archive large amounts of content. Through revenue sharing arrangements we are also generating resources needed to bolster media performance in Africa.'[173]

He said most countries in Africa with reasonably strong economies now have a variety of media available – there are at least 250 daily newspapers across the continent. However, where political openness and stability lag, the media suffer and journalists still face death and imprisonment. There are major questions to be asked about political control of the media in many

---

[172] http://opengovernance.info/BTKenya/.
[173] http://cima.ned.org/in-the-news/america-gov-allafrica-founder-cites-explosion-of-independent-media-in-africa.html.

countries and the degree of editorial independence which exists.

However, the internet provides a continent-wide distribution platform which can reach beyond national influence and control. Salim Amin runs A24, an online news distributor, which takes material from journalists anywhere in Africa, verifies and if necessary repackages the material, and sells it on their behalf to other African media or the rest of the world. 'I initially wanted a Pan African TV channel', he says, 'but I couldn't get the funding. In hindsight the online model is better. I don't think this would work without full integration online and especially with mobile.'

Afrigator.Com is a social media search engine and blog directory for African content with functionality that allows users to customise the site to offer the subjects, countries or conversations they are interested in.

In Nigeria, SaharaReporters.com combines aggregation with more of a watchdog role. It has an aggressively free speech agenda, publishing stories which local news agencies avoid, and many see it as close to muckraking. However, as one commentator observed:

> *If there were transparency in the matters of government*
> *and business, the need for Sahara Reporters would be moot,*
> *but in the absence of the freedom, boldness and courage of*
> *mainstream Nigerian media to report on controversial issues*
> *that expose people in power as unrepentantly corrupt but*
> *masquerading as respectable; a bit of guerrilla reporting as*
> *championed by Sahara Reporters is welcome and should be*
> *encouraged until things begin to improve in Nigeria.[174]*

Then there are activist sites like Sokwanele.com. It is run by a group (possibly financed in the West) dedicated to undermining Zanu-PF and Robert Mugabe. It is part of a network of political exiles and underground activists who ensure information about abuses of political freedoms and human rights are shared. In 2008 it acted as a hub for election results supported by pictures and SMS messages from the public seeking to prevent vote rigging. In a country where state control of the media is high, it is an exceptional example of public networking and information in its own right – as well as a valuable source for anyone wishing to report Zimbabwe. The internet has allowed journalism within and about Zimbabwe to revive in the face of internal crackdowns on traditional media.

These are examples of fresh confidence in African journalism which can be expected to develop and grow rapidly. There are many initiatives to support such development, ranging from the African Media Development Initiative

---

[174] http://akin.blog-city.com/nigeria_ribadu_and_kids_get_bundled_out_of_nipss_graduation.htm.

(AMDI),[175] arising from the 2005 Commission for Africa, to the Highway Africa Project,[176] to a range of journalism training schemes. The African Media Leaders Forum which meets annually has projects designed to promote editorial standards, to offer consultancy and mentoring for the private sector and to support capital investment in media and journalism.

The pressures African journalists work under are real of course. Consider the Editor of the *Zambia Post*, Fred M'membe, repeatedly arrested, attacked and intimidated by the government but determined to stand firm for press freedom in Africa.[177] Or Andrew Mwenda, founder of *The Independent* in Uganda, supporter of free speech and economic empowerment, charged with sedition in 2005 and frequently arrested since.

There are significant political and economic constraints on free and independent media and many risks still associated with outspoken journalism. Yet the spread of mobile phones and the internet is opening up debate and free reporting – and a range of coverage which is beginning to push its way through to Western media. News organisations are increasingly recognising the opportunity and importance of Africans reporting Africa.

Philip Gourevitch, who has reported from Rwanda over the last 15 years, explains:

> *In 1995 ... to get in touch with Rwanda from New York you used the phone – and there was no mobile network and landlines were scarce. That left me to scour the international press – which has never been a consistently reliable or reliably consistent source of daily information about Rwanda, because nobody reports on the place at a very high level or with any great frequency, except when there's a crisis. And when there's a crisis that's the story and it often eclipses any deeper insight into context. With time, as email and the internet became ubiquitous, I have had many more sources to consult – and it's been far easier to stay in more regular contact with a broader range of my own sources when outside the country. Best of all, the internet has given me access to the African press – local, regional, continental whose take on things is interestingly often very different from the Western press which basically ignores the African press view of Africa.[178]*

[175] http://downloads.bbc.co.uk/worldservice/trust/pdf/AMDI/AMDI_summary_Report.pdf.
[176] www.highwayafrica.com/.
[177] www.freemedia.at/singleview/4977/.
[178] Interview with author, Sept. 2010.

For foreign correspondents to consistently report more than the headline crises of famine and war, Africa has to have a public space where it can support the discovery, development and distribution of a wide range of stories. Technology is providing this and, in spite of old problems persisting, a fresh agenda for Africa is opening up which international reporters are recognising.

The continent provides many examples of the ties between political, economic and media strength and freedom, now all being driven by access to technology. While the West is locked in a debate about the crisis in journalism, across Africa the debate is about new forms of journalism asserting themselves in a strengthening economic and political environment.

9. Iran: Reporting a Closed Society

Interconnection is not presence (Roger Cohen)

Reporting from Iran has always been a challenging assignment – particularly for Western reporters since the Islamic Revolution in 1979. It is a closed society with tight controls over foreign media – and over those wishing to speak to the media. At times of crisis (like the 2003 student demonstrations or the post-election protests in 2009) the authorities crack down even harder both on the media and on the demonstrators. Yet it is also a highly connected and literate society with high levels of internet use. In 2008 it was estimated that about 22 million people in Iran were connected to the internet, with approximately 65,000 blogs.

For reporters whose movements are seriously restricted within the country – or others trying to report Iran from outside its borders – social media have become a means of finding out what may be happening and gathering pictures, information and firsthand accounts. Yet it can be no substitute for the core responsibility of the correspondent to bear witness to events and report firsthand. Some organisations have employed Iranian journalists to report for them, making use of their contacts and deeper understanding of a complex society as well as the lighter restrictions on their movements. However this can run the risk of them or their families coming under political pressure or threats if the authorities are unhappy with their reporting.

Nazila Fathi is an Iranian journalist who from 2001 to 2009 reported for the *New York Times* from Tehran. She understood it was a position that brought some risk with it.

> *During periods of turmoil, I learned to lie low and report what I could, through a screen of warnings that some things – demonstrators' slogans, even executions that had been announced domestically – were too sensitive to be reported outside Iran. But I thought the Iranian government were learning to tolerate us.*

She was wrong, and after a series of threats to her and her family she fled to Canada. Many of her friends and almost all her sources were thrown in jail. When she left, she feared her understanding of Iran would be frozen at that moment and she would be unable to keep up with events from the other side of the world.

> *Three things made all the difference: the global reach of the internet; the networking skills of exiled journalists and our sources; and the resourcefulness of Iran's dissidents in sending information and images out. In fact by following blogs and cellphone videos seeping out of Iran in some ways I could report more productively than when I had to fear and outwit the government.*[179]

Pooneh Ghoddoosi of the BBC's Persian TV service has an example of such reporting. Early in 2010 they heard reports of six separatist Kurds being hanged. They later heard one of them was a teacher and found pictures on the internet of him building a school. Without access to lawyers or family but with contributions from their audience they pieced together the story of the six men which was at odds with the official version. The story attracted attention and grew and they managed to produce a second programme about them. None of this would have been possible from within the country.[180]

The BBC's Persian TV service has made a virtue of reporting through the contributions – pictures, emails, SMS texts, letters – from their viewers. They are forbidden to report from within Iran. At the height of the post-election protests they were receiving eight video clips or pictures a minute from within Iran. The relationship has brought them closer to their audience and provided the TV service with a sense of authenticity about what they report, but it comes with problems. First, everything has to be verified. They try to contact those who contribute before using the material or cross-reference the material with other information and pictures sent in.

Secondly, the bulk of the material is sent by young pro-reformists, which leaves them with the problem of how to balance the views they broadcast. Sometimes they simply have to caveat their broadcasts, making it clear the views they carry may not be representative of public opinion throughout the country. However, building a regular network of trusted contributors has enabled them to report Iran – without those contributions they could not. They have to accept that such sources and blogs can change rapidly. 'If I go on leave for two weeks the first thing I do when I get back is update my sources

---

[179] 'The Iranian Exile's Eye', *NYT*, 16 Jan. 2010.
[180] Interview with author, June 2010.

because 30 per cent will have vanished or changed' says Ghoddoosi. [181]

Bob Tait was the *Guardian*'s Iran correspondent for three years until he was expelled in 2007. He then reported Iran from neighbouring Turkey for another two years. The job became significantly more difficult after the 2009 elections. 'Many of the reformist papers have been shut and a lot of the contacts I used to call are either now in jail or are too terrified to talk. In fact people now just don't pick up the phone if you dial their mobiles when they realise it's a call from abroad.'

He monitored events through blogs like Rah-e Sabz (Green Road), Mowjcamp and blog forums like Balatarin until they were attacked by Iran's officially backed hackers known as the 'cyber army'. There were official sites too representing the regime, like the Iranian Parliament's site Parlamennews, or Khabar Online or Tabnak. He also agrees that in some respects it may have been easier to report the story from outside Iran than inside. 'The real problem has been primary sources. It's become very difficult if not impossible to speak directly with anyone involved in the unfolding situation.' He recognises this is profoundly unsatisfactory. 'You are basically feeling your way through the story. Misjudgements are bound to result from that.' One example is the Ashura demonstrations in December 2009. 'We know something dramatic happened that day. But we don't know the extent of it in terms of the sheer numbers or what kind of people were involved. It means it's hard to counter regime claims it was only small.'[182]

Jon Leyne, the BBC correspondent expelled in 2009, agrees reporting from a distance has risks. 'It's very intangible but you miss the atmosphere. You can't go to the end of the street and pick things up.' Roger Cohen of the *New York Times* was eloquent in reflecting on the core journalistic responsibility to bear witness:

> *To bear witness means being there – and that's not free. No search engine gives you the smell of a crime, the tremor in the air, the eyes that smolder, or the cadence of a scream.*
>
> *No news aggregator tells of the ravaged city exhaling in the dusk, nor summons the defiant cries that rise into the night. No miracle of technology renders the lip-drying taste of fear. No algorithm captures the hush of dignity, nor evokes the adrenalin rush of courage coalescing, nor traces the fresh raw line of a welt.*

[181] Ibid.
[182] Interview with author, March 2010.

> *I confess that, out of Iran, I am bereft. I have been thinking*
> *about the responsibility of bearing witness. It can be singular,*
> *still. Interconnection is not presence.*[183]

In the wake of the 2009 elections, Western reporters were tightly restricted and many expelled. Social media, in particular Twitter and YouTube, were widely celebrated for helping Iranians tell the world what was happening. The Web Ecology Project analysed discussion on Twitter for three weeks around the election.[184] They found:

- From 7 June until 26 June they recorded 2,024,266 tweets about the election in Iran.

- Approximately 480,000 users contributed to the conversation.

- 59.3 per cent of users just tweeted once – and they contributed 14.1 per cent of the total number.

- The top 10 per cent of users accounted for 65.5 per cent of total tweets.

- One in four tweets about Iran was a retweet of another user's content.

During the first two days of protests (11–12 June 2009) I closely studied what was being said on Twitter and arrived at this conclusion:

> *If you, as an average news consumer, relied on Twitter you*
> *might believe all sorts of things had happened, which simply*
> *hadn't (tanks on the streets, Opposition members arrested,*
> *the election declared void, students killed and buried ...)*
> *running a high risk of being seriously misled about events on*
> *the ground. You might, at best, have simply been confused.*
> *You probably wouldn't have thought Ahmadinejad enjoys*
> *much popular support at all.*
>
> *But if you had a reasonable understanding of social*
> *media, how to set up and assess feeds, how to compare and*

---

[183] www.nytimes.com/2009/07/06/opinion/06iht-edcohen.html.
[184] http://webecologyproject.org, 'The Iranian Election on Twitter'.

*contrast information, if you had a reasonable understanding
of news flows, a developed sense of scepticism, and an above
average understanding of the political situation in Iran,
you would have emerged much better informed than the
lay viewer relying on TV or Radio news. The information
online ran significantly ahead of the news organisations
(who hopefully were taking time to check what they could)
but it came at a high noise to signal ratio. ... (at one point I
measured almost 2500 updates in a minute – though usually
it was closer to 200).*

*Social media can be a huge benefit in news coverage –
not least it was one of the few ways for people in Iran to
communicate with the West. But mediation by people who
understand the story and don't have a particular agenda to
advance is still needed to get a grasp of what has, and hasn't,
actually happened and a measured sense of proportion. What
was evident on Twitter this weekend was the accelerating
effects of a continuous news cycle and appetite. Just as 24
hour news channels must stay on air with some kind of
coverage, social media is even hungrier. And noise fills the
void when events or facts can't.*[185]

Subsequently it was recognised that much of the Iran election coverage on Twitter was polluted by recirculating rumour as fact, users pretending to be in Iran when they weren't and deliberate misinformation. The vast majority of the conversation was conducted by users outside the country.

Miriam Meckel from the University of St Gallen has analysed the coverage by Robert Mackey of the *New York Times* during the Iranian protests.[186] As well as writing for the paper he reported on his blog and was active on Twitter – often recirculating and contextualising information from inside Iran. Her conclusion was that he relied on 12 sources, carefully chosen, and acted as a bridge between the social media audience (niche, specialist, acutely engaged) and the general readership of the *New York Times*. Social media became the source for his coverage – but was subject to all the usual checks and balances a journalist would use with any other source.

It is a role which has taken hold since, with few Western correspondents allowed into Iran. Specialist websites like Tehran Bureau and Enduring America become prized sources of information. Based in the USA, they

---

[185] Extract from my blog, 'Sacred Facts' (written June 2009): http://sambrook.typepad.com/sacredfacts/2009/06/twittering-the-uprising.html.
[186] http://cyber.law.harvard.edu/interactive/events/luncheon/2010/05/meckel.

aggregate and verify social media from Iran using their expertise to provide a rich diet of information in greater detail than any general news service.

Nic Newman in his paper on the impact of social media on journalism[187] quotes two verdicts on Twitter during the Iranian uprising. Andrew Keen, author of *The Cult of the Amateur*: 'Twitter is a great real-time tool for distributing opinion but it is no replacement for curated media coverage of the crisis.' And Mark Jones, Head of Communities for Reuters: 'Our job now is packaging raw feeds from many sources and filtering it to provide audience big enough to make a difference. It is all becoming more complex, for journalists who need to monitor a huge number of sources, and more complex for consumers too.' Both are right. What this reflects is the accelerated news cycle which is sped up further by the capability of social media to communicate in real time. However it has no more validity that any other word on the street.

Journalists still have the responsibility to verify, contextualise and explain – perhaps more than ever for a country as complex as Iran. If social media contributed to the breaking-news end of the editorial value chain then the need for sober professional analysis was even greater at the other end.

The demonstrations in June 2009, and the political crackdown which followed, demonstrated real limits to foreign correspondence. Western reporters were expelled or had their movements restricted. Local staff, on which many organisations had come to rely, were compromised. Social media were initially celebrated as a means of reporting the protests, but sober reflection revealed serious limits to their effectiveness. Clearly, in closed societies where there are few other means of gathering information, social media have an important role to play. But they are no substitute for professional journalism or, in particular, for bearing witness.

---

[187] *The Rise of Social Media.*

10. Case Study Conclusions

These three, very different, situations – China, Africa and Iran – have some elements in common.

- The 'crisis' in journalism seems to be a Western phenomenon. In Asia there is significant media expansion, albeit often with state backing. In Africa and other parts of the developing world journalism is establishing a stronger base off the back of growing economic and political stability.

- Social media are increasingly helping countries develop a public space for debate, the exchange of information and views and to tell their own stories where previously this had not been possible.

- Social media are helping foreign correspondents report those countries with greater insight and accuracy as well – but are not a substitute for firsthand eyewitness reporting.

- News organisations are showing an increasing reliance on local staff to help them report from difficult countries and to bridge cultural gaps.

- The skills of aggregating local content and verifying and interpreting it are becoming increasingly important.

- There is a need for greater specialism and training of journalists to accurately reflect complex stories across boundaries. In an interconnected world, international journalism needs to be better informed and more culturally aware than ever.

11. Conclusions

In March 2009 Mike Gudgell, the Baghdad bureau chief for ABC news, met a group of colleagues from other networks in the garden of the ABC compound. 'We could all see it coming,' he said. 'CBS was gone. NBC was cutting back. Fox was looking for a less expensive space and ABC was struggling with how best to move forward.' When he noted that this might be the end of the multimillion-dollar bureau, the others nodded in agreement. He said: 'It wasn't just the end for now. It was the end – period.'[188]

A judgement on the end of a time of expensive bureaux for Western news organisations – but not on international reporting altogether. Why should it be a surprise that the means of reporting the world, developed over the last hundred years, should collapse as the digital revolution takes hold? And why should it be a cause for alarm?

The news industry, always conservative about itself, is caught in transition from an analogue past to a digital future and is worried it will not survive the change. Many elements, like multimillion-dollar bureaux, will not. But much will, and there will be innovation and new opportunities to more than compensate for what is lost.

This process should not be left unmanaged however – particularly with the risks of a knowledge and digital divide among some audiences. What's important from the old world must be transported and reinterpreted for the new.

News organisations have been exposed to the full force of the market which has flushed out inefficiency, low productivity and cross-subsidies in ways which at times have been brutal but which needed to happen. At the same time digital technology has arrived, increasing the numbers of channels available, the tools available to journalists, and opening the public information space to many new actors besides news organisations.

Alongside these changes, globalisation has brought to bear a new set of cultural perspectives, which have challenged and undermined old assumptions

---

[188] Quoted in Marcus Wilford, 'The Big Story: Our Embattled Media', *World Affairs*, Fall 2009.

about reporting. Many newsrooms have been – and continue to be – slow to react to these changes, leaving innovation to come from outside the industry. Some of the consequences of this have been:

- The relentless closure of major news bureaux around the world – but investment in low-cost newsgathering and parachute reporting.

- Fewer staff correspondents based abroad – but greater opportunities for freelances and local staff.

- The arrival of 24/7 real-time news soaking up effort and resources – but more channels for reporting the world than ever before.

- A shrinking of professional foreign newsgathering – but an explosion of other sources of information.

- The commoditisation of some kinds of foreign news – but a new premium on breaking news and in-depth analysis which some organisations are turning into sustainable business models.

- A blurring of the foreign and domestic agendas and pressures on impartiality – but new global audiences seeking information relevant to their lives.

- A crisis in Western journalism – but growing confidence in Africa, China and other parts of the world.

So what are some of the changes to foreign correspondence we are likely see over the next few decades?

For most of the twentieth century, the average foreign correspondent was likely to be male, middle class, working with a high degree of independence to one or two deadlines a day, reliant on support from local staff in a well-funded bureau. They would be one of the few sources of information for their audience or readers at home, working with little transparency or accountability. Their network of sources amounted to dozens at best. They tended to be resilient, competitive individualists. They probably didn't speak the language of the country in which they were based or have many non-professional friends or contacts in the country but they would, over time, develop a degree of specialist expertise.

In future, foreign correspondents are likely to be far more diverse in gender, ethnicity and background. They will speak the language and have specialist knowledge of the country before they are eligible to be appointed. They may well have grown up there or lived there before. They will work to multiple deadlines each day across multiple media (text, audio and video), they will be heavily networked with other specialists and with public sources in their area of expertise. Their network of sources will be counted in the hundreds. Their brief may not be purely geographical, but subject-led as well. They may work for several different organisations as a stringer or freelance rather than being on the staff of one organisation. They are more likely to work from home. They will be addressing multiple audiences around the world and will be aware that they are not the only, or even main, source of information. Their role will be as much about verification, interpretation and explanation as revelation. As such they will need social and collaborative skills. They will take steps to ensure the way they work is as transparent as possible in order to win the trust of editors and the public.

For the last hundred or more years, the dominant news culture has been Western, led by Europe and the USA. In 20 or 30 years' time that may no longer be true – at least to the same extent. Western editorial values focused on holding power to account, conflict, confrontation, political pluralism, human rights, individualism, humanitarianism and liberalism may give ground to Asian values of deference, social harmony, respect for authority, welfare, collectivism – with a consequent impact on global news agendas.

Challenges

The challenges for professional news organisations looking at the future of international coverage have to be seen in the context of a transition from print and broadcast to digital and interactive news provision. In many respects we are still early in the process of that transition. However a number of issues seem clear.

Three roles

News is fragmenting. As the middle ground has fallen away from news coverage it increasingly leaves three roles for news providers:

- coverage of breaking news and live events,

- deep specialist niche content with analysis and expertise,

- the aggregation and verification of other sources of information.

Larger providers may offer all three of these categories, smaller organisations may need to specialise in one or two, but all news organisations need to decide which of these to offer.

Breaking news and broadcast coverage of live events remain staples of daily news and sources of competitive value. In addition, those organisations able to offer specialist expertise can find a lucrative niche audience by offering depth and expertise. Interest in feature and policy-led reporting is falling away. However, in future, news organisations should offer expertise in aggregation, verification and analysis of the torrent of new information and voices from outside the media industry which is affecting public debate. This will increasingly be a core role and requires fresh skills. The new voices are both source material for news organisations but also competitors for public attention. Newsrooms must recognise they can provide a valuable service by curating and filtering this information on behalf of their readers, viewers and listeners.

Rethinking the agenda

Foreign and domestic issues have merged in many cases – calling into question the geographical organisation of coverage. There is a demand for issue-led and specialist news from abroad. Audiences clearly respond to more of a 'bottom–up' agenda facilitated by interactivity rather than a purely government or policy-led approach. Lack of interest in foreign news may in part be fed by a lack of imagination or innovation in international coverage.

For the less well educated or wealthy there is the potential of a self-reinforcing spiral where they become less aware of, and therefore less interested in, international issues. News organisations, as they adapt to the 'separation' of news, need to make extra efforts to catch this group with personally relevant or engaging international reporting.

Broader coverage

The additional productivity of international reporting, facilitated by the falling costs of digital newsgathering technology, should be used to broaden the range of international reporting as well as increase the supply of a core agenda to an increasing array of platforms. This requires deliberate intervention and management of the news process. The default position is to supply the same news to ever more services. However, differentiation is increasingly important to attract audiences and international newsgathering can play a useful role.

Partnerships

Foreign news desks must adopt a more networked approach to reporting the news, taking advantage of the range of social media and other sites available, of the flexibility of the new digital freelances, local journalists and stringers.

Together these can provide swift expert response and analysis without the overhead of a major bureau and permanent staff. Managed in the right way they can complement the staff correspondents and provide a rich diet of relevant, reliable, informed news. News organisations will not be able to compete head-on with the speed and variety of social media – curation and partnership is necessary. As one Reuters editor put it, 'we used to need hunter-gatherers; in future we'll need farmers'.

Innovation

Even in a threatening economic environment, space and resources must be found for innovation. To purely defend the old models, approaches and routines will not ensure survival. Most of the innovation, around aggregation and data-led analysis for example, comes from outside professional news organisations. Although these services are seldom profitable yet in their own right, they are pointing the way to fresh approaches with significant consumer and citizen value.

New economic models

Original international reporting will never be cheap and may never pay its own way. However, it brings lustre and credibility to a news brand, the public clearly expect it as a core part of any news service and, most importantly, in an increasingly interconnected world it is a crucial element to understanding the domestic news agenda as well. Specialist organisations, particularly in the financial sector, can offer premium niche services to help subsidise overseas operations. Other news organisations need to use digital opportunities to find their own premium offer which can work in tandem with the less profitable parts of their news service.

Training and recruitment

In the long term, news editors must commit to greater professional training for foreign staff. All coverage is visible globally and domestic audiences are better informed about the world than ever. It is increasingly clear that language skills, cultural awareness and subject or country expertise are more important than ever for the accurate portrayal of international events and issues. Cultural gaps need careful bridging, but there are real advantages in the greater use of local staff. There is a new generation of internationally educated and experienced journalists who are particularly able to fulfil this role. British and American universities, for example, teach increasingly large numbers of foreign students who aspire to bridge continents and cultures in whatever work they do.

These are turbulent times for news organisations. Economics, technology and globalisation are proving difficult cross-currents to navigate. However, if we can cast off some of the assumptions of the past, and retain only what's necessary for the future, there are exciting prospects ahead. Some much valued aspects of foreign reporting from past decades may be lost, but the innovation and opportunity afforded by digital technology seems likely to herald a new golden age for those interested in reporting the world.

As Andrew Currah concludes:

> *In the short term, the craft and economics of professional journalism will continue to morph in new, unexpected directions – some of which will compromise the quality and availability of public interest news. In the longer term, there is scope for various forms of intervention by government, media businesses, and even by citizens themselves. The digital revolution may spell the end of the mass media age, but it also marks the dawn of a more participatory media age which promises both commercial and civic dynamism.*[189]

So are foreign correspondents redundant? By no means. But they will be very different from their predecessors and work in very different ways to serve the digital news environment of the twenty-first century.

Whatever the changes in expectation, technology, professionalism and skills, however, there is at least one respect in which they will be the same. Whatever the economics of international news, it is something which all news organisations must strive to preserve. That is, the responsibility to bear witness.

From William Howard Russell in the Crimea, to the beaches of D Day. From Baghdad, Kabul, the streets of Tehran or Tiananmen Square or the genocide in Rwanda, eyewitness reporting has been and will remain of crucial importance. There is no substitute for being able to say 'I was there and this is what I saw'. It is the heart of international journalism. In the words of the BBC's Allan Little:

> *Eye witness journalism is in one sense the purest and most decent work we do. It has the power to settle part of the argument, to close down propaganda, to challenge myth making. It is the first draft in the writing of history and, in itself, a primary source for future historians.*[190]

The independent witnessing of events has been the core purpose of foreign reporting from its earliest days and will remain so for the future.

---

[189] Currah, *What's Happening*, 159.
[190] BBC College of Journalism.

List of Interviewees

Salim Amin, CEO A24
Al Anstey, Head of Editorial Development, Al Jazeera
Philip Balboni, President and CEO, Global Post
Charlie Beckett, Director, Polis
Emily Bell, *Guardian* (now Columbia Journalism School)
Deborah Bonello, *Financial Times*
Marcus Brauchli, Executive Editor, *Washington Post*
Tyler Brule, *Monocle Magazine*
Kathleen Carroll, Executive Editor, Associated Press
He Dalong, Bureau Chief, Xinhua
Mahmood Enayat, Oxford Internet Institute and BBC World Service Trust
Pooneh Ghoddoosi, Presenter, BBC Persian TV
Philip Gourevitch, *The New Yorker*
Carrie Gracie, BBC Correspondent
Ibrahim Helal, Al Jazeera
Graham Holliday, Freelance journalist, Kigaliwire.com
Mark Jones, Global Communities Editor, Reuters
Joel Kibazo, former journalist, FT, Reuters, BBC
Jon Leyne, Iran Correspondent, BBC
Allan Little, BBC Correspondent
Chuck Lustig, ABC News
Rebecca MacKinnon, Princeton University
Sean Maguire, Editor, Political and General News, Reuters
Richard McGregor, *Financial Times*
Andrew Mwenda, *The Independent* (Uganda)
Turi Munthe, CEO Demotix
Vincent Ni, Oxford Internet Institute
John Owen, Al Jazeera and Professor of International Journalism, City University
David Schlesinger, Editor-in-Chief, Reuters
Harriet Sherwood, Foreign Editor, *Guardian*
Vaughan Smith, *Frontline*

Robert Tait, Iran Correspondent, *Guardian*
Marcus Wilford, ABC News
Jon Williams, World News Editor, BBC
Ethan Zuckerman, Berkman Centre, Harvard

Bibliography

Adie, K., *The Kindness of Strangers* (Headine, 2002)

Alleyne, M., *News Revolution* (Macmillan, 1997)

Beckett, C., *Supermedia: Saving Journalism so it can Save the World* (Blackwell, 2008)

Bell, M., *In Harm's Way* (Penguin, 1995)

Blundy, D., *The Last Paragraph* (Heinemann, 1990)

Bowen, J., *War Stories* (Simon & Schuster, 2006)

Boyer, P., *Who Killed CBS News?* (Random House, 1988)

Bromley, M., and T. O'Malley (eds), *A Journalism Reader* (Routledge, 1997)

Buerk, M., *The Road Taken* (Hutchinson, 2004)

Bunce, M., 'Reporting Dynamics and Cultural Clash at an International News Bureau in Nairobi', *The Round Table: Commonwealth Journal of International Affairs*, 99/410 (2010), 515–28.

Carey, J. (ed.), *Faber Book of Reportage* (Faber, 1996)

Castells, M., *Communication Power* (Oxford University Press, 2009)

Cudlipp, H., *The Prerogative of the Harlot* (Bodley Head, 1980)

Currah, A., *What's Happening to our News* (RISJ, 2008)

Danner, M., *Stripping Bare the Body* (Nation, 2009)

Davies, N., *Flat Earth News* (Vintage, 2009)

Doctor, K., *Newsonomics* (St Martin's Press, 2010)

Downie, L., and R. Kaiser (2002) *The News about the News* (Random House)

Evans, H., *War Stories* (Bunker Hill, 2003)

Evans, H., *My Paper Chase* (Little-Brown, 2009)

Gellhorn, M., *The View from the Ground* (Granta, 1989)

Gourevitch, P., *We wish to Inform you that Tomorrow we will be Killed with our Families* (Picador, 1999)

Gowing, N., *'Skyful of Lies' and Black Swans* (RISJ, 2008)

Hamilton, J. M., *Journalism's Roving Eye* (LSU, 2009)

Hamilton, J. M., *Reporting from Faraway Places: Who Does it and How?* (Nieman Reports, Harvard, Sept. 2010)

Hannerz, U., *Foreign News* (University of Chicago Press, 2004)

Hargreaves, I., *Journalism: Truth or Dare?* (OUP, 2003)

Hastings, M., *Editor* (Macmillan, 2002)

Hess, S., *International News and Foreign Correspondents* (Brookings Institute, 1996)

Kershaw, A., *Blood and Champagne: The Life and Times of Robert Capa* (Pan, 2002)

Knightley, P., *The First Casualty* (Andre Deutsch, 2003)

Lippmann, W., *Liberty and the News* (Transaction, 1920)

Loyn, D., *Frontline* (Penguin, 2005)

McGregor, R., *The Party* (Allan Lane, 2010)

Marr, A., *My Trade* (Macmillan, 2004)

Matheson, D., and S. Allan, *Digital War Reporting* (Polity, 2009)

Miles, H., *Al Jazeera* (Abacus, 2005)

Okrent, D., *Public Editor* (Public Affairs, 2006)

Owen, J., and H. Purdey, *International News Reporting: Frontlines and Deadlines* (Wiley-Blackwell, 2009)

Pavlik, J., *Journalism and New Media* (Columbia, 2001)

Pax, S., *The Baghdad Blog* (Atlantic, 2003)

Perlmutter, D., and J. M. Hamilton, *From Pigeons to News Portals* (LSU, 2007)

Sambrook, R. (ed.), *Global Voice* (Premium, 2007)

Simpson, J., *A Mad World My Masters* (Macmillan, 2000)

Smith, A., (1979) *The Newspaper: An International History* (Thames & Hudson)

Snow, J., *Shooting History* (Harper, 2004)

Sperber, A., *Murrow: His Life and Times* (Freundlich, 1986)

Tomalin, N., *Reporting* (Andre Deutsch, 1975)

Tunney, S., and G. Monaghan (eds), *Web Journalism: A New Form of Citizenship?* (Lewes, 2010)

Webster, F. (ed.), *The Information Society Reader* (Routledge, 2004)

Whittemore, H., *CNN: The Inside Story* (Little-Brown, 1990)

Acknowledgements

I would like to thank all of those who agreed to be interviewed by me for this project – all were extremely generous with their time and thoughts. I would also like to thank the staff and Fellows of the Reuters Institute for their support and advice – particularly David Levy, James Painter, Geert Linnebank and John Lloyd. Richard Addy at the BBC was generous in helping with audience research and conclusions – conducting most of the analysis. John Owen of Al Jazeera and City University and David Weinberger of the Berkman Centre made acute and helpful comments on early drafts. Graham Holliday was a constant source of ideas. My new colleagues at Edelman were supportive and influenced a number of the thoughts here, particularly Robert Phillips, Steve Rubel and Richard Edelman. My wife and children deserve many thanks for their patience while I completed this study.

There are many aspects of the new world of foreign reporting and new global information flows that were beyond the scope of this study. They include a robust analysis of the reduction in numbers of correspondents and quantity of coverage; analysis of past and current diversity among reporting staff; analysis of the changing international news agenda; comparison of the agendas and content of social media sites and traditional news sites; comparison of different language content; the impact on coverage of newsroom organisational changes; fuller analysis of global information flows beyond the media – and more. However I hope this high-level review has at least provoked some new thoughts and perspectives. Needless to say all mistakes are my own.

Finally thanks to my colleagues and others that I met during 30 years in BBC journalism, for the comradeship, conversations and shared experiences which unwittingly shaped this report.